A PRODIGY

My Secrets at Southern University and
Agricultural & Mechanical College,
Year One

ELIJAH J. D. PRECCIELY

Foreword by
Dr. Jesse B. Bilberry, Jr.

Royalty Publishing

A Prodigy

My Secrets at Southern University and Agricultural & Mechanical College, Year One

By Elijah J. D. Precciely

Published by Royalty Publishing
Ponchatoula, Louisiana
Royaltypublishing04@gmail.com

This book or parts thereof may not be reproduced in any form, stored in a retrieval system, or transmitted in any form by any means – electronic, mechanical, photocopy, recording, or otherwise – without prior written permission of the author, except as provided by United States of America copyright law.

Unless otherwise noted, all Scripture quotations are taken from The Holy Bible, King James Version, KJV.

Visit the author's website at www.AProdigyTheBook.com

Copyright © 2020 by Elijah J. D. Precciely.

All Rights Reserved.

ISBN: 978-0-9991626-7-5
Printed in the United States of America

ELIJAH J. D. PRECCIELY

My Experience, Observations, and Advancements!

A PRODIGY
MY SECRETS AT SOUTHERN UNIVERSITY AND AGRICULTURAL & MECHANICAL COLLEGE, YEAR ONE

My Honor and Gratitude

My appreciation and thankfulness are first to my Heavenly Father, my Savior Jesus Christ (Yeshua, the Messiah) and my best friend: The Holy Spirit of God. God has given me the ability and support to accomplish and achieve all tasks and assignments for His glory. I thank God for my family. To My dad, mom, sisters, brother-in-law, nieces, the Whole Precciely Family, My grandparents, Thank you for all the love, faith, prayer, wisdom, discipline, and support you have given me and for consistently loving and seeking God first. I love you!

I am particularly appreciative of my university, scholars, staff, faculty, contractors, administrators, board members, my Scotlandville community, East Baton Rouge Parish, the city of Baton Rouge, the state of Louisiana and all institutions of learning and higher learning. I am thankful for each person who has dedicated their lives to impart knowledge to family, friends, and strangers. To all those who have supported me in Corporations, Media, Politicians, and Entrepreneurs, Thank you.

In addition, I am extremely grateful to all the ministries and people who support them. Especially to those who have been an example in using their gifts, talents, skills, and abilities to serve, edify and increase the body of Christ for the Kingdom of God and His Righteousness. I admire you for not hiding your talent(s) in the ground and for being as bold as a lion. To my entire church, jurisdiction family and ALL my instructors: You have shown and continue to demonstrate to me the way I should grow. May you continue to greatly impact the lives of this generation and future generations with your knowledge, laughter, and LOVE. Amen!

The Foreword

In my years as a pastor of Mount Pilgrim Baptist Church, I had many wonderful experiences. I never shall forget the day in 2010 when the churches of Scotlandville (located in North Baton Rouge, Louisiana) all came together for Prayer and Praise on the Bluff. It was on that day I became acquainted with Pastor Stephen D. Precciely, his lovely wife and family, including the author of "A Prodigy," who was only three years of age at that time.

My fellowship with Pastor Precciely has been on the increase since we met, and it did not take me long to observe that Pastor Precciely and his wife were parents with a Kingdom Agenda, and their children were being reared in the nurture and admonition of the Lord. They were their children's first teachers, following God's instructions, and God's unfailing law in Proverbs 22:6, "Train up a child in the way that he should go: and when he is old, he will not depart from it." Their curriculum came from Deuteronomy 6:1-9. The school was known as "The Mother's Knee." As these parents follow God's instructions, then God can prepare Elijah for the mission He has called him to do on his earthly sojourn.

Then, thank God, when his mother discovered they were blessed with a prodigy in the house, she carried him to Southern University, the place where God had prepared to take care of him. Thank God for Southern University, my bridge over troubled waters. Growing up in Farmerville, Louisiana, I thought Southern University was the only

A PRODIGY
MY SECRETS AT SOUTHERN UNIVERSITY AND AGRICULTURAL & MECHANICAL COLLEGE, YEAR ONE

university in the world because my father was a graduate of Southern, and his words were always "Not IF you go to Southern, WHEN you go to Southern." He was incredibly positive. I am the oldest of 10 siblings and we all followed our father and graduated from Southern University. In 1969, I returned there and worked in Student Affairs until I retired in July of 1984. I was Director of Admissions when the enrollment exceeded 10,000 and maintained for several years on the Baton Rouge Campus.

Since the age of 8, Southern University has been providing opportunities for Elijah to grow; Now (at the age of 13), after completing his first year of college as a full-time student, he has written a book entitled "A Prodigy," sharing his secrets, experiences, observations, and advancements…And what a book it is! It is indescribable! The table of contents contains 12 chapters using the 12 letters found in the word I-N-S-T-R-U-C-T-I-O-N-S. In the first 2 paragraphs of the book, he expresses gratitude to his Heavenly Father, his family, and his university. He then talks about the importance of knowledge. He quotes Hosea 4:6 "My people are destroyed for a lack of knowledge." He is a student with a plan! This book has so many outstanding features. "Order Your Day" just blows me away! I recommend this book to high school students, potential college students, families, and all who want to be fruitful. Follow INSTRUCTIONS! What a way to go! It will be interesting to see what another year will bring for Elijah!

Reader, if you will notice the author has quoted Scriptures time and time again, and he has constantly expressed gratitude to his family. He talks about putting God and His Kingdom first and all these things shall be added unto you. The family is God's foundational institution. Every other institution is built and predicated upon the family. If the family breaks up, then those institutions that depend on strong families break up as well. Once that happens, there is no law that you can pass that will make up for the devastation. There is no program you can institute that will fix what happens to people's lives when a home is shattered. There is no politician you can elect who can bring harmony and social order when the family is decimated.

    I pray that the author will share this publication with the Admission Office because what Southern University is doing for him, it can do for others!

    I say unto you Brother Elijah, "Let no one despise your youth, but keep on setting examples," 1 Timothy 4:12 and keep on Matthew 6:33ing!!!

Dr. Jesse B. Bilberry, Jr.

Southern University Class of 1951

Pastor Emeritus, Mount Pilgrim Baptist Church

A PRODIGY
MY SECRETS AT SOUTHERN UNIVERSITY AND AGRICULTURAL & MECHANICAL COLLEGE, YEAR ONE

Table of Contents

Introduction
   Our Knowledge has a History 16
   Purpose Fueled Choices 30
   To Build or To Destroy 37

Chapter 1:   **I**nstructions Irradiates 48
Chapter 2:   **N**ever Dumb Down 55
Chapter 3:   **S**tudy with Results 62
Chapter 4:   **T**uition Cognition 70
Chapter 5:   **R**elentless Resources 77
Chapter 6:   **U**nderstanding Unlimited 91
Chapter 7:   **C**heating Extirpates 95
Chapter 8:   **T**echnology Transcends Time 102
Chapter 9:   **I**nitiate to Ignite Change 110
Chapter 10: **O**pportunities are Options 119
Chapter 11: **N**ot Ready? – Think Again! 124
Chapter 12: **S**ystem of Instructions R.O.C 129

Gold Bricks 138
My prayer for you 139
References 142
About the Author 144

A PRODIGY
MY SECRETS AT SOUTHERN UNIVERSITY AND AGRICULTURAL & MECHANICAL COLLEGE, YEAR ONE

Introduction

"Within the finest designs, well-built structures, and magnificent works is the demonstration of knowledge.

The Gold Bricks of Instructions lay at the foundation of every great work."

"There is a Knowledge, which is not ephemeral, it lasts forever!"

For I Am A Child

This is what Elihu, son of Barakel the Buzite, said:

"I'm a young man,

and you are all old and experienced.

That's why I kept quiet

and held back from joining the discussion.

I kept thinking, 'Experience will tell.

The longer you live, the wiser you become.'

But I see I was wrong—it's God's Spirit in a person,

the breath of the Almighty One, that makes wise human insight possible.

The experts have no corner on wisdom;

getting old doesn't guarantee good sense.

So I've decided to speak up. Listen well!

I'm going to tell you exactly what I think." Job 32:6-10 MSG

    I know some people consider me as just a child. I should only be seen and not heard, or I should only be used by adults for entertainment, sports, or their personal gain.

    Elihu said it well. God bless children and those who are young to show and to speak to those who are not. Elihu, Samuel, David, Jeremiah, the lad with the two fishes and five barley loaves of bread, and Jesus were all children empowered by God to give messages to families, communities, and the world.

Yes, I am very young to attend such a Great University.

Knowledge at all levels is profound! Being accepted at any age for the purpose of expanding knowledge at increasingly higher levels is remarkable! To be in an atmosphere to draw from individuals who have embraced learning and want to creatively help advance the knowledge of others is brilliant, magnificent, and a privilege!

There are uncertainties; however, I am given this confidence, my university and I will excel to do great and supernatural exploits. You may ask why or how I can make such a statement. It is said, when you touch the heart of a child, you touch the heart of God. My heart has been touched and God is true to his word:

"And Whoso shall receive one such little child in my name receiveth me. But whoso shall offend one of these little ones which believe in me, it were better for him that a millstone were hanged about his neck, and that he were drowned in the depth of the sea." Matthew 18:5-6

Matthews 25:40 says, "And the King shall answer and say unto them, Verily, I say unto you, In as much as ye have done it unto one of the least of these my brethren, ye have done it unto me."

I am one of the least of these, for this reason, I know God will continue to bless us in every area of our lives because this is being done unto Him!

A Prodigy is only the beginning of an invested array of pertinent secrets of wisdom, knowledge, and understanding from my first year in college. I am honored to share the abundant and copious wealth from my unique journey to pave the way for others.

Provided inside these pages are some of my well noted experiences, observations, and advancements to help you prepare for college and show you how to excel with knowledge, if you are in college.

It is a privilege for me *to do more* with what I have been given. It is a privilege *to...*

Maintain,

Improve,

Increase, and

Share what I have.

Excitement is stirred when we give favor, opportunities, and blessings to others. Giving releases intense and accelerated blessing in our lives, begins greater cycles of opportunity, and increases us more and more, and our children.

To pave the way for others, in each chapter are strategies I am confident will advance you forward, as you persevere through all schooling and life.

I begin with where knowledge is found...

ELIJAH J. D. PRECCIELY

Knowledge is found inside of

I. N. S. T. R. U. C. T. I. O. N. S.

Instructions ARE the way of Life!

If you want better in life,

follow the instructions,

betimes!

Initial Instruction: *Remember the best way to learn is with Faith and Love!*

Our Knowledge has a History

As a full-time scholar, I am ecstatic to finish my first year of college. The colleagues I have met are some of the BEST-ever. I am pleased and thankful to be a part of "The Jaguar Nation."

The largest land-grant for a Historically Black College and University in the world is... "The Southern University and Agricultural & Mechanical College." As the third generation and the third sibling in my family to attend a University, I realize knowledge and higher learning **must be** EXTENSIVELY celebrated in our communities.

Founding President Dr. J. S. Clark and Dr. Booker T. Washington along with other leaders at Southern Univesity - c.1915

My grand mommy had a slogan she would say with a smile, "It is a poor frog who won't praise his own pond and every crow should think his nest is the best and his chicks' feathers are the blackest, riches, fullest and healthiest." My grand mommy is definitely right. Not only praise and celebrate the pond, but also the fish, the frog in the pond, the land around the pond, the houses near the pond, the city, the state, and the crow. With immense admiration, my university was established in April 1880 in New Orleans, Louisiana. We are celebrating over 140 years of educating people to impact our world. To educate a person for one or five years is important, but over 140 years is incredibly astounding.

It was the collaborative efforts of Great men who were legislatures (Theophile T. Allain, Erick J. Gilmore, Henry Demas, and former Governor Pinckney Benton Stewart Pinchback) who petitioned the State Constitutional Convention in 1879. At the time, Louisiana had three private colleges, Straight University (1868), Leland University (1870) and New Orleans University (1873). Southern University started educating (12) twelve scholars in a four-bedroom house with five faculty members and a budget of $10,000 [1]. It was an official college, in a "Praying" homeschool for college setting. As a bit of seldom mentioned but a very true part of our history: Our legacy of education and building higher institutions of learning was steeped deep in prayer, the word of God, and the church. Good Success was inevitable.

In 1890, our university relocated to 512 acres on Scott's Bluff in Scotlandville, located in North Baton Rouge, Louisiana [2]. The first president at the Baton Rouge location was James Samuel Clark, for whom my scholarship, J. S. Clark Scholarship was named.

Our history is absolutely incredible! Understanding the commitment to knowledge and education amazes me to this very day. I have wondered if our founders knew the great changes they were initiating. Do you think they had people like myself in their minds knowing we would appreciate this university so much? If so, I am glad they thought enough of me to pursue this great feat despite the obstacles! This is proof, what we do now matters for innumerable people in the future.

The Skull and Bones Scientific Society was formed to stimulate interest and encourage higher scholarships in the Scientific Department at Southern University (STEM) – Scholars in photo taken 1929[3].
http://www.subr.edu/page/little-known-facts

The reconstruction era from 1865 to 1877, reminds us that we can do the impossible, when we are united. Today, Southern University Systems consist of five institutions or campuses located in the state of Louisiana. They are as follows: The Southern University Law Center; Southern University, New Orleans; Southern University, Shreveport; Southern University Agricultural Research and Extension Center; Southern University, Baton Rouge (My Campus). The President-Chancellor is **Dr. Ray Belton**; the Vice-Chancellor and President of Academic Affairs is **Dr. James Ammons**; the Senior Associate Vice Chancellor for Academic Affairs is **Dr. Bijoy Sahoo;** and **Dr. Dialo Bagayoko**, the Distinguished Professor Emeritus of Physics, Distinguished Dean Emeritus of the Delores Spikes' Honors College and Distinguished Director Emeritus of the Timbuktu Academy.

I am more than elated to attend this great university. I applaud other scholars with similar opportunities. It is obviously a tremendously bold exploit. It requires a prodigious extent of support to be accepted into college. The S.U. family is supporting and encouraging me throughout my college career into my Doctorate. This endeavor is completely self-less. To attend any college at my age is phenomenal, but to have the endorsement of my entire university is opulent.

From left to right: **Dr. D. Bagayoko; Dr. J. Ammons;** *"Future Dr."* **E. J. D. Precciely; and Dr. R. Belton**
The Great Gentlemen are in the order of appointed encounter.

We Still Stand on the shoulders of GREAT visionaries.

Dr. Anthony Stewart of the Physics Department, thank you for teaching me how it is important and okay to stand on the shoulders of GREAT people, especially in learning.

These GREAT men have help to change the world, and this includes my life as well:
My Dad, Pastor Stephen D. Precciely;

Dr. Munir Ali (English);

Professor John Alleyne (Theater: Graphics Design);

Dr. Albolfazi Amini (Engineering);

Dr. Donald Andrews (Dean of Business);

Dr. Shawn Comminey (History);

Dr. B. Craig (Engineering);

Dr. Walter Craig (Engineering);

Dr. Patrick Carriere (Dean of Sciences);

Dr. Ken Ford (STEM Research);

Dr. Fulu (Abuja, Africa);

Dr. Feng Gao (Physics);

Professor and Coach David Geralds (Health);

Dr. Michael Garrard (Law Center);

Dr. "G" Ghebreyesus (Economics);

Dr. Emmitt Glynn (History);

Dr. King David Godwin (Speech and Theatre);

Dr. Laurence Henry (Physics);

Mr. Floyd Hodu (Computer Science Recruiter);

Dr. Samuel Ibekwe (Engineering);

Dr. H. Dwayne Jerro (Engineering);

Pastor and Dr. Andre Johnson (Agriculture);

Dr. Conrad Jones (Chemistry);

Dr. E. Khosravi (Computer Science);

Dr. Runell J. King (Enrollment and Recruitment);

Dr. Fred Lacy (Engineering);

Mr. Christopher Levy (Financial Aid and Scholarships);

Dr. Eduardo Martinez (Biology);

Dr. Stephen McGuire (Physics Emeritus, Nobel Prize in Physics);

Dr. Patrick Mensah (Engineering and MBA Research);

Dr. Thomas Miller (Foreign Languages);

Mr. Isaiah Norwood II (Computer Science Recruiter);

Mr. Jason Ordogne (Information Technology);

Professor Sherman Pitman (Business);

Professor Eric Pugh (Honors);

Dr. Terrance Reese (Physics);

Dr. Anthony Stewart (Physics);

Professor Archie Tiner, Jr. (Architecture);

Dr. C. Rueben Walker (Agriculture);

Dr. S. Washington (Chemistry/Engineering Camp C.E.E.S. "Center for Energy and Environmental Studies");

Bro. Clovis. R. Williams III (STEM Mentor);

Dr. Ashagre Yigletu (Business MBA); and

Dr. G. L. Zhao (Mathematics and Physics) just to name a few.

"Knowledge does not end.

Learning must not end.

Keep learning at all costs!"

A Paradigm Kairos:

It is not a Dictate; it is a Mandate!

    I have embarked upon a powerful and extraordinary journey of immeasurable wealth for a lifetime. Let me start with Friday, May 25, 2018 (even though our miraculous journey of my life starts well before I was born). I sincerely thank God for both of my parents and my supportive family. If my parents were not obeying God for my life, this would be vastly different. I am the blessed to be a blessing.

    It was announced to the world that I accepted status as a "full-time" college scholar with a "full-ride" scholarship to Southern University and Agricultural & Mechanical College. Excited and ecstatic was an understatement. Although I was so pumped for the complete and fully encompassing levels of opportunity to do great exploits, this was not entirely new to me. I have been attending college courses from 8 years of age thanks to the wise and profound guidance of Dr. Bagayoko and permission from my parents.

    This all came about when I was creating and building things at my house. I would take things from all around the house like pots, pans, cleaning items, chemicals, detached items as well as take apart my toys. Whatever I could find, I would create and build something new. I love to invent and think about inventions, innovative ideas, and solutions all the time. My mom did not quite know what I was consistently up to each day. She became especially concerned when I began asking for high-powered magnets and liquid nitrogen. Mom knew she needed help and began to seek after more knowledge.

One Friday morning as scholars were returning to School, she said to me, "Get ready, we are going on campus to meet the Dean of the Physics Department and Honor's College, Dr. Diola Bagayoko, to get help." So, we met in his office. I was sitting in the chair listening to the conversation somewhat. Then, the Dean requested to talk with me. He asked several pedagogical questions and listened intently to my dialogue. After the complete Socratic analysis (evaluation), he informed my mom, "He needs to start attending classes, NOW!" Well, my mother was the founder and principal of an entire school, but she understood the beginning phases of the many uncommon and unique, but necessary sacrifices.

Since I am sharing an extremely condensed measure of my story, I will let you in on one of my K.E.Y.s. Most children like me do not need to be stagnated, …, in the counsel of limiting mediocracy, …, or put-off; we just need all our creative energy to be ingeniously redirected with …, and consistent results.

From that time on, and without interruption, I began attending 2 to 3 courses each semester. My courses were and continue to be fantastic and remarkable. My new experiences in knowledge began opening an abundant world of excitement. I have entered more levels and areas of learning with people who understand and help expand my dialogue and ideas. My university is perfecting and is filled with godly purpose.

As part of my school requirements with Ji'L Academy of Beyond Excellence, I had to actively volunteer once a week. Thanks to Mrs. Tamara Montgomery, who I met at a career fair, I began my first volunteerism with Career Services of Southern University. A portion of my task included interacting with various department deans, professors, and distinguished visitors on campus. My awesome opportunities with Career Services were professional and prominent. More scholars should experience and learn the gift of volunteering. My parents taught me volunteering is a seed of giving your time that will harvest into increased blessings.

My job was speaking with companies, meeting new people, helping set up events, promoting and working the career fair. I also had the opportunity to work with different people in the career services such as Mrs. Kathy Hayes. I was doing what I enjoyed, which is sharing knowledge, getting to know people, engaging in conversation about STEM ideas, and dressing professionally...just like the 8 Cardinal Values from Professor George Washington Carver. I would attend the career fair every semester accompanied by my mother.

I had a purpose-filled desire to be a full-time scholar, but I did not know how my college would be paid for at my age. For me, I knew being in debt was not an option. I asked the Lord about where I should go to school and for a scholarship. I also knew before enrollment, I would be required to follow state and university standards (i.e., instructions) including, but not limited to, all documentation and standardized testing.

Well, the spring career fair of 2018 was exceptionally different by far. As I was walking around in the arena, seeing so many colleagues, introducing myself and conversing with individuals from various corporations, I met Dr. James Ammons. He was the newly appointed Vice Chancellor of the University. Dr. Ammons complimented me on my suit, asked my name and asked about me. Then the conversation began. I introduced myself to him, "I am Elijah J. D. Precciely," and explained I was attending a couple of classes from the age of 8 years old under the tutelage of Dr. Bagayoko. I informed him the classes were only used for my high school credit. I was not getting college credit and could not receive financial aid to help me enroll in a 4-year university, due to my age. When this was brought to his attention, he was amazed. He wanted me to continue my education at Southern University and went to work right away. During this time, I received letters from other universities, but God already spoke to my heart about Southern University.

> *Believe and know, consistency in following instruction does not go unrewarded.*

By the middle of May, we received a special call from Dr. Kimberly Fergurson-Scott, who was over student affairs. I was delighted, thrilled, and honored all at the same time. She asked to set up a meeting with me and my parents to talk about stipulations and my offer of a full-ride scholarship!!!!!!! My faith vision was being revealed.

The gifted individuals I initially received innovative instructions from deserves Double Honor. It takes a unique genius to recognize various levels of genius.

Now and in the future, there will be more scholars similar to myself. These scholars must be recognized early, before they are institutionalized and limited in their creativity. Only select universities will be prepared and ready with diversity and understanding of what to do and how to manage giftings. With Dr. D. Bagayoko, designated professors and administrators, "My" Southern University is ready with opportunities and resources!

When our historical life changing opportunity was set and signed (May 25, 2018) one of the most important things I said was *"And I will absolutely pave the way for others to do the impossible."* This came directly from my heart and not my notes. Inside of me, the response was astounding. I knew at that critical juncture that a scripture was even more real to me. "To whom much is given, much is required." I must share instructions with those who will hearken or in Hebrew language the word is '**shema**' (which means, "to listen to do.")

Many millions of people around the world are academically excited for me, my university, and the opportunities of hope it brings for others with unique gifts. I have postured myself with help, prayers, and support of those who will join me to create opportunities to pave the way to positively increase, improve and change our world. With the entire-real truth of knowledge guided by instructions, people can be free from the chains of lies, anger, poverty, fear, and destruction.

Historical opportunities present themselves when we follow the standards of instructions!

ELIJAH J. D. PRECCIELY

At every level, phase, and stage, Knowledge is a choice. Right choices are not limiting.

Purpose Fueled Choices

> *"The Right Choices create Order, Obedience, Options and Overflow."*

My choice for College Knowledge, immediately made me a College Entrepreneur. When we think like an entrepreneur, we are...

- innovative to develop a clearer vision and refine ourselves.
- to grow in value and worth of what we have to offer.
- to decide and appreciate our assigned location and areas to impact.
- to understand and manage our increase and influence.

With the support of my sister-teachers, who are life-long learners, I learned about product, price, place, and promotion, respectfully before college.

I made My Choices in Knowledge

"Some may think, what physicists and engineers do is a stretch of the imagination." I am fully persuaded it is the knowledge of God working through creativity. In my research, engineers may think, design, or create an ingenious project with the ability or power to produce a physical machine, idea, or concept to better society. The Hebrew slaves in both Egypt and America were great physicists and powerful engineers. They worked to make their lives easier and produced while creating from a simple idea or vision. An engineer has an innate desire to build or create. I believe scientific knowledge is added to perfect the skills of the engineers.

I have watched and studied engineers all my life. From the beginning, I have always loved to design, build, and create using anything inside and/or outside of the house. I would make something better, create something to play with, change my surroundings, and think through challenges. One main act of engineers is the capability to be thinkers and communicators who change the world from dialogue into creation. This knowledge makes me more committed to helping human conditions. I will share and provide information on my inspiration, infrastructure and innovativeness which has motivated me to be a perfect engineer.

To be completely clear, my inspiration has not come from my family or the idea of money. My inspiration is what was given to me as long as I can remember and even now. I was given stories from the Bible where engineers were clearly depicted. These stories are not just fairy tales - they are of individuals who designed, created, and used things without modern technology, nor anything from a textbook. It only came from God. First, there is the story of Noah. God told Noah to build this BIG Ark. Noah was given the **instructions** on the measurements of the Ark. It should be over 515 feet in length, over 85 feet wide and about 51 feet in height. So, God made Noah an Engineer. Noah would be considered a Structural, Materials, Mechanical and Interior Design Engineer. Next there is King Solomon, the wisest man who ever lived; He was an engineer and physicist. God **instructed** him to build one of the most iconic and greatest structures in history. This marvel was of marble, gold, silver, precious stones, and great works of brass and jewels. This great marvel of engineering was the Temple of the Lord known as Solomon's Temple. It has a length of over 100 feet. Solomon's Temple was over 33 feet wide and was constructed to be over the baffling height of 198 feet.

Today, a person cannot make a life size model of this unless it is made of Styrofoam. It would still cost a great deal. The Temple of the Lord, built by King Solomon and his men, used only the finest materials of an era. These include: Cedar wood, Copper, Gold, Cypress, and a plethora of other rare materials of an era. Solomon's Temple or the Temple of the Lord was completely covered with pure gold! The ranges of skills needed were from Materials to Interior Design Engineering.

Another inspirational person was Nehemiah. He was given instructions to repair and rebuild the breach in the wall that surrounded the city. Given that he used his engineering skills to properly repair and fix the damage wall, one can say Nehemiah was a Civil Engineer. Noah, King Solomon, and Nehemiah were all Management Engineers, those who managed the work and progress of others to complete the original idea or vision given to them (by God).

According to the Bible Jesus' earthly father was Joseph, the carpenter. Joseph taught (instructed) Jesus the skills of carpentry, which is called a Construction or Fine Arts Engineer. Jesus was a master builder; he built everything from houses to furniture. He would make marvelous works of wood. Aside from building structures, most importantly, Jesus Christ had the capability to build up the lives of people who accepted him as their Lord and Savior.

Like Noah, King Solomon, and Nehemiah, I am absolutely confident that I have been created to be a physicist and mechanical engineer focusing on all the sciences and aviation. Why? Because God has plans, purposes, and projects for me to create, solve, and fulfill. Some of which can only be fulfilled through being a Physicist and Mechanical Engineer.

My infrastructure of being a Physicist and Mechanical Engineer begins with my family. I am not the first person in my family to be an engineer or inventor. My foundation includes many different types of engineers.

For example, on my *maternal* side, my great-grandfather was a self-made Mechanical Engineer and a Materials Engineer working with wood. My grandfather was a self-made physicist; general contractor and civil engineer who even redesigned and built our family home. My grandmother was considered an Interior Design and Fabrication Engineer. My great uncles Buddy, Otis, and cousin Dean Eddie H. were types of engineers. My uncle Carlton earned his degree in Electronic and Computer Engineering and became an Aerospace Design Engineer. My mother studied computer programming and became a System Quality Assurance Analyst Engineer who analyzed and evaluated business computer systems. My sister and brother-in-law have both studied Electrical and Mechanical Engineering, respectfully. On my paternal side, both of my uncles Rick and Jim are Electronic Engineers. My paternal grandfather was a self-educated Mechanical Engineer who would rebuild amplifiers and created a cooking device using the car motor. Because of his idea, they would cook food under the hood of the vehicle while on the family road trips. "Fast Food on the Go!"

Although I was around so many engineers, I was able to narrow my interest to Physics and Mechanical Engineering because of my inventions and innovative ideas. A Mechanical Engineer designs, develops, research, manufactures, and tests all types of devices. They may test mechanical devices, power products, machines, electric generators, internal combustion engines, gas turbines, work on power heated seats, refrigerators, air conditioners, equipment machines tools, material handling, airborne robots...in my opinion Mechanical Engineers are the key to society. Without mechanical engineers, there would be no magnetic rail trains, no robots, no refrigerators; there would be no microwaves, and, saddest of all, no Frosted Flakes or at least they will cost a whole lot because all the manufacturing would be done by hand. Most of the products we enjoy would not exist. To sum it up in one quote, "Without Mechanical Engineers, there may be feet, but there would be no shoes and without Physicists there would be no understanding of why our shoes remain on the ground."

> *"Engineers are Master Builders and Physicists are Realm Masters."*
> *Brianna P. Craig*

Knowledge has History, an Attitude, and a Thirst; however, there is a Lack of Knowledge and there are Blockers.

The Best Knowledge Commands Respect, Revelation, and Continuation.

To Build or To Destroy
Does knowledge Build or Destroy?

Our Attitude for Knowledge

My sister Brejena, who is a genius and graduated in Marketing Sales and Management at age 20 from Southern University, often shares this quote from Henry Ford, "Whether you think you can or you think you can't, YOU ARE RIGHT." I have always been aware that knowledge will bring increase, but it is our attitude towards knowledge that allows us to earn a position or place of consistent revelation.

In the words of Dr. Bill Winston, "Information without revelation is stagnation and devastation." It is like having a Rolls Royce without the wheels. The vehicle cannot be applied or used. I call this information certified, but not applied.

Unlike before college, full time college scholars have a decision to make. The decision must be made whether they want to be here to learn and increase in knowledge, or if they just want a passing grade, maybe a job, and not a career for their years of half-hearted commitment. You cannot be afraid to allow yourself to do more to have good success. It is a decision.

Everything flows in the direction of your decision. I decided to learn. In the true words of my dad's great friend (therefore, my friend), Pastor Jesse Blakey, "When you decide, you kill and cancel all other options." Knowledge is an option. It can be accepted or rejected. I made my decision. I have chosen to enjoy learning good knowledge. The more I learn, the more I want to learn. Now at Southern University, I have been provoked to augment my learning and matriculate in knowledge. I want the precious knowledge and information that may be undervalued by others but is tremendously imperative. With knowledge I can do more to help myself and others.

Our Thirst for Knowledge

It has been recorded that George Washington Carver would go to his laboratory every day. He Called it, "God's little-workshop." Carver would take his Bible into his laboratory every time. He would consistently ask for direction. Professor Carver would teach his scholars the 8 Cardinal Virtues [4], which I value as I thirst for knowledge.

With the right knowledge first, you can do even more to make a difference in our world. And when we build on the knowledge and join with the right people resources, we can do magnificent and magnanimous exploits. I am persuaded for every problem there is a solution. To be the cutting edge of knowledge is a reward for those who are assiduous with the knowledge they are privileged to learn and apply.

"Learn like your life depends on it because it does!"

George Washington Carver's 8 Cardinal Virtues

1st   Be clean both inside and out.

2nd   Neither look up to the rich or down on the poor.

3rd   Lose, if need be, without squealing.

4th   Win without bragging.

5th   Always be considerate of women, children, and older people.

6th   Be too brave to lie.

7th   Be too generous to cheat.

8th   Take your share of the world and let others take theirs.

"May God help you carry out these eight cardinal virtues; and peace and prosperity be yours through life."

A Lack of Knowledge

It is true, some people are afforded the choice for knowledge. And some are not privileged to access knowledge, while others simply reject knowledge. Yes, there are consequences, and our societies reflect this truth.

I have learned a plenitude of information and knowledge during my first year. I have also learned, there is a great price to pay for a lack of knowledge. I must reflect. When I was younger, I would generally hear people quote the first portion of the scripture from Hosea, chapter 4, verse 6, but would not quote the entire scripture. It reads, *"My people are destroyed for lack of knowledge"* but as you read further the scripture tells us why *"because thou hast rejected knowledge, I will also reject thee…"* It is clear, a lack of knowledge not only causes damage, but it causes people and things to be destroyed. Because knowledge has been *rejected, resisted, refused, scorned, excluded, prohibited, unwanted, eliminated, forbidden and disregarded*, we are all affected.

The word destroyed means to ruin, put out of existence; annihilate; impoverish; vanquish; to ruin as if by tearing to shreds. Can you imagine the negative impact we have if we reject knowledge? Sometimes people stop learning and applying knowledge after college and often after the master's or PhD degrees. Even after accomplishing success in life, we must always keep learning. You should never quench the fire or fervor for knowledge. We should learn and create knowledge. The negative effects are deeper than imaginable. To have or be in a deal with a person who lacks knowledge is uncomfortable at best. If you are required to interact with a person who does not want to grow or learn is frustrating. Rejecting knowledge is so painful. It is like deeply hurting your best friend or someone who really loves you time after time. This type of recurring pain and cycles of suffering exist as long as the knowledge is being repudiated and disregarded. Let that sink in for a minute or a lifetime.

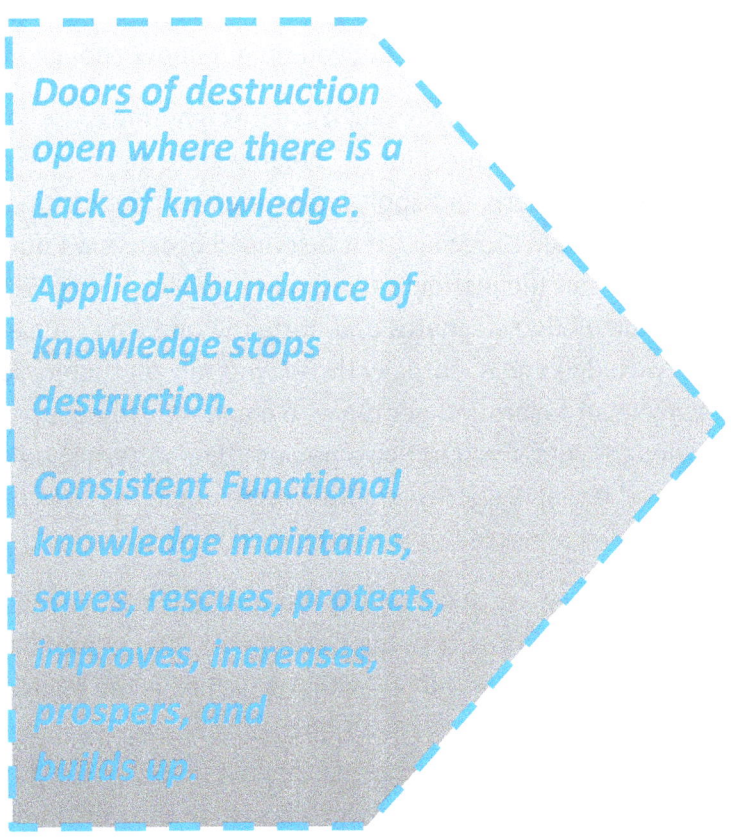

Doors of destruction open where there is a Lack of knowledge.

Applied-Abundance of knowledge stops destruction.

Consistent Functional knowledge maintains, saves, rescues, protects, improves, increases, prospers, and builds up.

The Blockers of Knowledge

You may ask, what blocks a person from accepting knowledge? Some knowledge blockers are: unforgiveness, negativity, anger, roots of bitterness, hatred towards others, age and gender discrimination, past and present hurts; and unresolved pain. All these can be wrapped into one, Pride. Pride is a definite blocker of knowledge. Pride says, "I already know; I do not need your help; who are you to teach me; I do not want you to tell me anything; I do not need to know that; you cannot tell me what to do; you do not know enough yet."

When knowledge is blocked, it creates ignorance. Ignorance stops advancements. When we are given an opportunity to learn and apply knowledge, but are obstinate, it is detrimental. Especially, if it is refused because we do not like the person the instruction or knowledge is coming. The lack of knowledge stagnates and hurts the one who refuses the knowledge and eventually those who rely on them. *Note to self:* Never be around people who constantly reject or stop knowledge. And if you notice a person's life pattern should be better, it may be because somewhere down the road they or someone connected to them rejected knowledge.

Each time we are given an opportunity to learn, we must embrace and cultivate it to our betterment. Our present and future depends on it. Did you know, teaching is the highest form of love? (Hebrews 12:6-11; Proverbs 13:24) Teaching is love and to learn is to reciprocate the love. So, you must have a kind heart to receive knowledge. It says to the person or instructor who is giving the knowledge, I trust you. The Spirit of love must be the driving energy to receive knowledge.

Our Best Knowledge

The Hebrew word for knowledge is **ya'ath**, meaning perception, skill, discernment, understanding, wisdom, and awareness.

When it comes to knowledge, according to the Benjamin Bloom's Taxonomy, there are four (4) categories [5] of knowledge:

1. Factual Knowledge

2. Conceptual Knowledge

3. Procedural Knowledge

4. Metacognitive Knowledge

The first two types, **factual** and **conceptual**, constitute **"knowledge of what."** The last two types, **procedural** and **metacognitive**, constitute **"knowledge of how to."** Similarly, factual, and procedural knowledge constitute low level knowledge whereas conceptual and metacognitive high-level knowledge.

The best type of knowledge has existed forever. People have spoken of this knowledge for years. I would hear people say, "Something told me, I had an unction, I was warned, I heard in my knower." Then I have heard people say, "Do not ask me how I know, I just know." Well, after the crucifixion of Jesus Christ (Yeshua Hamashiach) on the cross, Jesus spoke of a comforter, who would come. He is the Holy Spirit of God to dwell in us once we accept Christ as our savior, the Messiah. We have been promised a unique teacher, a comforter, and guide.

This is called **Revelation "Grace" Knowledge that comes directly from the Spirit of the Lord God Almighty**. *(Thank you, Dr. Bill Winston).* As an accomplished Professor, George Washington Carver demonstrated Revelation Knowledge through his works. When asked what he takes into his laboratory, he called God's little workshop? The answer was only one book, the Bible.

Revelation Knowledge allows believers in Christ Jesus to understand to manifest solutions. Solutions that will impact the world when we receive them. Did you know, when we follow instructions, the Holy Spirit of God feels welcome to give us "The next?" I decided to follow instructions to receive God's Knowledge called **Revelation**.

ELIJAH J. D. PRECCIELY

Continue the Respect...

Our Respect for Knowledge

The best judgment is to respect knowledge. I have noticed during my life, some people think it is okay to know just a little, and others refuse and reject learning after they achieve (whether it is a high school, college, or doctoral degree). We all have opportunities to learn.

My grandfather would say to me that "Everybody is important, and everyone is a doctor (potentially) in their own right." This is so very true. Learning and applying Biblical concepts can be gained from everyone. My interaction with others has taught me what to do and what not to do. **Everyone has value**, but they must be willing to respect knowledge to develop it and themselves. God is never brutish as to why he has allowed us in the earth realm. He certainly has a purpose and a plan.

As I am growing, my mom would remind me of how challenging things were to carry a baby, especially with difficulties. I know I am not here by accident, and neither are you. It is an absolute that we are here for **a purpose**. We start by increasing our value through knowledge. Now, I would just add to my grandfather's quote, "Everyone is a doctor in their own right, if they perpetually choose to pursue knowledge." Knowledge is a choice.

Our Continuation of Knowledge

Learning must not and cannot end at the point of acquiring a degree. Capability is demonstrated by the achievement; however, we must not stop learning. A person can attend college and yet live like they refused to retain the knowledge acquired. All the knowledge, application and the increase must stay in operation.

There are those who go to school out of duty and just simply get a degree to be appeasing. Then there are those who understand the purpose for education, gain the knowledge, and are applying what they have learned but they refuse to stay abreast and increase their wealth of knowledge. For this reason, people who keep using old information and methods without incorporating or replacing it with new knowledge get left behind. Wow, this is something to think about whether they are a scholar or educator. Personal development is critical.

Through all the accomplishments, historical achievements, and the advancements in our society, there had to be instructions to guide each success.

> **"Knowledge is only ephemeral when memorized, we must persist to increase the longevity of knowledge by retention."**

Chapter 1

I – INSTRUCTIONS IRRADIATES

"Wise people listen to wise instructions."

"I Repeat...Wise people listen to wise instructions."

One definition of the word irradiate is to illuminate by or as if by shining light on it. Merriam-Webster says it best, "to <u>enlighten</u> intellectually and spiritually." Instructions, directions, guidelines, teachings, commands, and advice should irradiate as in clarify, expose, and reveal to increase one <u>Intellectually</u> AND **Spiritually**. The more we increase in wise instructions, the more we learn about how fearfully and wonderfully we have been made. We are made to increase.

Our intellectual and spiritual increase is awakened and incited. Great instructors, speakers, preachers, orators, educators, and those who speak with sound wisdom do not drive you from knowledge. On the contrary, they stir up a greater desire for more instructions to pursue even greater knowledge. I am thankful for my increase in wise instructors, who are scholars.

It is absolutely true; **A scholar is a life-long learner.** A life-long learner is both a person with profound knowledge and one who is <u>in pursuit</u> of profound knowledge. It is immensely interesting and exhilarating when I am given the opportunity to meet profound knowledge face to face. I see a joy and excitement of wisdom inside their eyes waiting to be poured out through instructions, like a shining light. It is as if I am meeting a portion of myself, filled with a wealth of knowledge that belongs to me anticipating the very point of impartation. Each instruction is a wealth transfer impartation and I want to learn and apply all I can from them.   I am a Scholar!

You can be a student by default, but it is far better and profitable to be a scholar on purpose. <u>A scholar receives wise instructions and applies the knowledge gained for profitable impact</u>.

Remember: A scholar is a learned person or one who pursues greatness in learning standards in a particular subject or in unlimited fields of study to holistically impact multiple aspects of life.

You should declare it for yourself, "I am a Scholar."

Scholar, just Follow the Instructions!

I am reminded of a test given to each scholar in pre-college school. The teacher told us we had 2 minutes to finish the test. There were about 10 problems. Before we started, she said, "Follow the Instructions." Needless to say, some of the scholars immediately began to answer the questions to complete as many as possible before the time was up. A few of us read the instructions which told us to simply sign our name and turn in the test. The test was worth 100 points. Some of the scholars could not believe how others were turning in the test so fast and receiving the 100 points. Here is the real reality and truth: *"He is in the way of life that keepeth instruction: but he that refuseth reproof erreth."* A proverb from the Bible located in Proverbs 10:17.

Wise instructions will <u>save</u> you <u>time, money, direct you to your success</u> and can even <u>save your life</u>. Scholars are trusted to do and have more when they can follow instructions. The difference between most scholars who succeed and students who fail is simply being compliant verses obdurate with following instructions. I have noticed some students at conferences, schools, community activities who seem to want to ignore, procrastinate, argue, create their own or distort the instructions or assignments given as if they were giving themselves the grade or assessment.

Instructions are the bridges that convert power to movement. Instructions are the switches to turn on and access how to use the power of knowledge.

Both simple and high-powered computers run by instructions (called commands). To successfully accomplish Math is to follow the steps and series of rules made of instructions. Physics ask questions of WHY and answers based on How-Instructions. To bring solutions to problems, there are instructions. To be an entrepreneur with a successful business, there are instructions. To fully operate or repair an online device, autonomous vehicle or lift-aircraft, there are instructions. To show a friend or team member how to do something, there are instructions. You cannot catch, grow, clean, or properly prepare food to eat without instructions. To be healed and stay healthy; and to acquire and maintain wealth, there are instructions. To relax, to work, to play, to live, to prey, to pray or to achieve your desires all require instructions. You cannot build or keep a house without following instructions. Even with creativity and to produce any good thing, you must have instructions.

The generational acronym for the B.I.B.L.E. stands for Basic Instructions Before Leaving Earth and Believing Instructions Betters Life Existentially.

Your brain (command center) voluntarily or involuntarily; immediate or delayed release (such as DNA to hormones) is instructing your body's functions. As Professor Tanganika Johnson instructed us to demonstrate, everything down to the cells of your body runs on instructions, either generating, transferring, translating, reprogramming, repairing, fixing, redirecting, or executing instructions.

Some people want to get away from rules, guidelines, direction, and do not want people to give them instructions on what to do or what not to do, but the older you get the greater the responsibilities and the more the instructions. With more creativity, there are more instructions.

A system functions by instructions, the less instructions the less the function. Bad or good, they are all instructions. One thing to note, a person's capabilities, flexibility, talents, or the creativity of instruction depends on the individual. The most intuitive things require instructions. Sad, but true, there are those who do not have to follow instructions in this way of life. There are 4 people who do not follow instructions:

1. The Living Fool
2. A Rebellious Person
3. A person lacking understanding and
4. A person without life

Wise People listen to Wise Instructions!

Scholar, Following Instructions Build Trust!

One of the first strategies to be successful in college and in life is to "Follow the Instructions." When I receive instructions from my professors (authority, leaders and yes, my parents), I just do it. I notice the options to procrastinate, make excuses and so on, but I remember to just follow the instruction, "When they are given," I have more peaceful time to do my uninterrupted research. If you did not understand the instructions from your professor the first time, *ask for clarity (shine more-light or enlighten)*.

When I was being schooled at home, my principal would not allow us to make the statement, "I need help." We were <u>instructed</u> to ask for clarity with a specific question or area. This procedure allowed us to think of what we really wanted to know, and not general whining help to avoid thinking. We were guided to formulate the question with the portion we received or understood into the question to show our buy-in or commitment to learning. Be specific, so people can help you better and faster. This will help in all areas of life.

We must remove the shame from scholars when asking questions and teach how to ask specific questions to move them forward. If you are not quite clear, ask for the instructions again or the portion you actually need. Always ask and seek how to advance and move forward. Always listen carefully to instructions. I find most people who give instructions do not mind repeating them if a person really puts forth the effort to want to learn.

What separates you from average and mediocrity is your commitment to consistently follow instructions and ask questions. Questions lead to answers which leads to instructions. So, always ask questions to get instructions to move forward. Knowing WHAT to do is your best plan. Most people who follow instructions are probably smart but, all those who refuse or do not follow instructions are absolutely choosing to be ignorant.

==Remember, "If people stop giving you instructions, **you are in a <u>bad</u>, <u>bad</u>, <u>bad</u> place of low expectations."**==

Finally, and above all else...**READ, READ, READ, READ, READ** to the 7th power!

Please READ your instructions, all of them. However, if you read and you do not understand, read it again and again. I have discovered it is more than alright to read and re-read it again. Just make sure you get an understanding.

"EACH INSTRUCTION IS **POWER**" which moves you forward with accuracy to the NEXT level of instructions!!!

In the words of the late Minister Gary Burks, "What did God say?" It is all about instructions. Instructions are both simple and complex. Instructions are simple (for even a child) when you follow them. They become complex when you ignore, delay with attitude, twist, or distort, omit a portion, argue, make excuses, do it wrong or procrastinate the instructions.

Here is a **Gold Brick**, even when you are in prayer, what you are really looking for are "Relationship Instructions." The Holy Spirit of God is my best friend. In other words, instructions are entrusted to you because of your consistent relationship with God. Therefore, during prayer (and you will pray while acquiring more knowledge) you should just get quiet and listen. After prayer, yield yourself to listen (throughout the day) for the instructions of "What God says." Then Hearken or Shema, which means listen to do!

Be a Scholar, "Look for the WISE Instructions that irradiates, then you must SHEMA!"

Chapter 2
N – NEVER DUMB DOWN
"Never Let Go of Your God Given Vision!"

Already I have heard, "Never, say Never." Usually, it is pertaining to an absolute when someone wants to be arrogant and put others down. Well, I can say confidently there are some "Nevers" we should remember in this chapter of success.

There are people who have said, "You really do not need college," but the truth is - knowledge can NEVER BE TAKEN AWAY from me and there is NO TIME LOST when I INVEST IN MYSELF. It is also an honorable privilege to be in the arena of like-minded individuals who can impart *(the professors)* and those who are ready to receive knowledge *(the scholars)*.

The Bible clearly states in Proverbs 9:9, "Give instructions to a wise man, and he will be yet wiser: teach a just man, and he will increase in learning."

Here is what I want **the wise** to remember with this next strategy.

1. **Never** forget where you came from and the people who have guided you along the way. Be thankful to those who have been and continue to be kind to you. Your life may have been their ONLY assignment to fulfill. Make sure they are appreciated.

2. **Never** reject or give up on you. Help has arrived. Sometimes when I present my ideas, they are out of the box or too big for some people to grasp. This can be exasperating. It is best remembered in a daily confession my mom received from Bishop and Dr. Houpe for our lives.

"Great people are ready to help me at the right time, and in the right way.
Some people may not even know it yet! I promise I will never give up.
God has resources that I may not have even considered. Sometimes it may seem like I do not have the help. I will trust God to provide. He will provide!"

According to Psalm 37:5 "Commit thy way unto the Lord: trust also in Him, and He shall bring it to pass." and Galatians 6:9 says, "And let us not be weary in well doing: for in due season we shall reap, if we faint not."

3. **Never** assume when you can confirm and be sure. Just search it out to confirm. Assurance works best to avoid redundancy in schoolwork, task, assignment, arguments, and projects.

4. **Never** take for granted you know everything when you do not. Be humble and learn. In the words of my mom, "You are not here because you know it all, you are here because you can learn it all." Enjoy the learning!

5. **Never** be ungrateful, it is the genuine test of increase.

6. **Never** start doing something you know will not prosper you. Be circumspectly prudent! Prevention is better than the cure.

7. **Never** think knowledge is a waste of time because <u>you are not a waste</u>.

8. **Never** forget there are more people praying for you than those who want to prey on you. You are surrounded by a great cloud of witnesses.

9. **Never** forget you can always be realigned; mistakes can be turned into miracles.

10. **Never** forget there are people who have been assigned to help you. They are waiting for you on the other side of each instruction and congratulation to move you forward.

11. **Never** think you are too young, too old, or too busy to begin your God given plan and fulfill your purpose. Purpose is given before birth and revelation of your vision is given while in pursuit to fulfill your purpose. So, start now!

12. **Never** be ashamed when you trust God. Expect God to move on your behalf. He WILL redeem you!

13. **Never** forget God will give you people who will think on a higher frequency or higher level with you. They may be few, but they DO exist. There are people who still exist who believe for the impossible and make it possible.

14. **Never** think you are alone. There are people cheering for you. They are happy you exist and excited about your success. But remember to encourage yourself to <u>do what is right</u> and not what is just good at the time.

15. **Never** be jealous or envious of others. You are also uniquely gifted. Begin celebrating and complimenting others. It is laudable to encourage others. It adds to your success and character. We are all a part of a great team, so every part is needed.

16. **Never** believe you are unteachable, you are actually gifted and created to learn. Because of your gift, choose your learning wisely and be very careful what you learn from negativity.

17. **Never** think you cannot understand. Gaining understanding is your decision to pursue. It is how information is effectively communicated. You must seek out great communicators who eagerly love sharing their creative explanation of information and knowledge.

18. **Never** agree with anyone who may say knowledge is powerless for you. These words and attitudes are usually from those who have been unthorough, incomplete, unfinished or they have not effectively used what they have acquired. Knowledge received and applied changes the world around you.

19. **Never** tolerate education that is void of creativity, BE RESPONSIBLY CREATIVE with your education.

20. **Never** think educational concepts that are rushed come from the educators alone. Use your skill to draw from other resources. Take your time to learn, and love learning. You can learn!

21. **Never** accept hindrances to your success, it is your choice to enter the dark side or remain in the abundance of peace with a higher frequency of light. Be aware and monitor your frequency of peace.

22. **Never** believe solely because a person is knowledgeable, that they can teach. Educating others is not just a skill, it is a gift.

23. **Never** give up your ability to judge between right and wrong, it is a great tool for learning and gaining wisdom to discern difference.

24. **Never** think small. Your imagination is the seed that will bless your life. So, practice thinking BIG; write your visions; and keep big ideas before you. You have been allowed to receive a glimpse of the end from the beginning.

"Since God IS "I AM,"

He is the reason for your success,

never forget him.

He will never stop blessing you."

Beware: There is such a thing as dark knowledge.

The worst situation is an educated individual that does not know and retain the sovereignty and greatness of God in their thinking and imagination. This is dark knowledge.

"Scholar, Never Dumb Down Equals

Do Not forget God!"

Chapter 3

S – STUDY WITH RESULTS

"When you learn, you increase your life.

Practicing is K.E.Y. to Mastery."

Each time you see the word **K.E.Y.** or an actual key,

I would like you to always remember,

"THE RIGHT **K**nowledge **E**difies **Y**ou!"

The question may be asked. So, why is studying so fundamental to a scholar's success? Most students want to succeed academically, but some may not have the desire to put in the work to study.

In the words of Dr. D. Bagayoko,

"You cannot just be a student; you must be a Scholar!"

Studying must consist of practice. In other words, practice is required to succeed. But not just any kind of practice, the result yielding practice. If indeed studying is imperative, how can we make the most of practicing? What MUST BE examined and analyzed is centered around these three questions:

1. Does studying increase academic success?
2. How can different study habits affect productivity?
3. What type of practice yields greater results?

Studying does increase academic success.

However, the way you study can increase or decrease its benefits. For example, "Distracted studying" is almost worse than not studying. If a person studies distracted, they do not accomplish much work at all. Studying that can increase academic success greatly is "focus studying." My mom said, "The longer you put off studying the longer it takes." The longer a person thinks about studying without any preparation or takes little action, the longer it will take. With focus study, it is better for a person to set study times and focus on one task until finished.

How can different study habits affect productivity?

There are many different study habits [7], some include: "Cramming;" "Distracted studying;" and "Practice Study." "Cramming" is where you try to do all your work in one day or a few hours without stopping for anything. But "Cramming" is incredibly hard to do in the eleventh hour with effective results. The faster a person goes without sufficient practice, the higher the level of mistakes. With "Cramming" there is not enough time to be thorough in studying. Thus, "Cramming" does not lead to long term learning. "Distracted studying" as I mentioned, takes a longer time to finish subject matter with gaps in learning knowledge and often leads to cramming. "Practice studying" yields greater results. "Practice studying" is when you practice for more than an assignment, but in general you practice ahead of time. You will learn and understand the subject matter better. This is particularly useful whenever there is a pop quiz, test and more importantly a presentation. You may also practice after each lesson and practice for mastery.

What type of practice increases productivity?

The type of Practice which produces greater results is the Power Law of Human Performance [6] developed by my Hogan, Dr. Diola Bagayoko of Southern University and Agricultural & Mechanical College and native of Mali, Africa. *(Mali, Africa is the place of the first University school of Higher learning, Timbuktu.)*

In summary, "If you do a task (complex or basic) a repeated amount of times with smaller amounts of time between intervals of practice, the better you become." The Power Law of Human Performance yields itself quite useful. For example, the more you practice writing or composing literature, the better you become. This works for all subjects. The Power Law of Human Performance is the most effective method of practice. *Note to self: You must read his entire research 7 times. Ask Ms. L. Franklin, M.S. for the link.*

"Practice is the result of someone who perseveres."

Daily practice in studying is vital because it drastically increases performance in school and in life. Focus your thinking around studying to increase academic success; your most effective and productive study habits; and your practice which yields the greatest results. Remember, according to the Power Law of Human Performance, the more you do something, the better you become at that task. For this reason, scholars who repeatedly practice a subject matter, excel greatly beyond their non-practicing counterparts.

A suggestion to Pre-College Educators:

My proposed solution is to share information about practicing the Power Law of Human Performance in studying. This information can be taught simply by teachers giving incremental tips to scholars on how to study. By teachers sharing information on crucial studying skills, this will help eliminate cram; distracted; and many other ineffective styles of studying. Successful techniques of studying are vital to our educational system in cultivating genius.

1. *By educating teachers about the Power Law of Human Performance*, teachers will be able to prepare scholars how to study effectively. This can be accomplished by devoting an entire class for study training or devoting time from a lecture in the curriculum to speak on study habits. The method should be introduced in elementary and continue throughout college. The solution of the Power Law of Human Performance will not take much time or resources from the current curriculum. By teaching scholars successful study habits, you increase their efficiency, speed and results in learning and retention which outweighs the time cost.

2. *How would instructors know what study styles the scholars are using?* The first scenario is studying as a part of the curriculum. The teachers will know the study styles because the Power Law of Human Performance is self-evident. The scholars' improved grades and attentiveness would reflect their study method. The second scenario is studying as a class. The professor would provide training on the Power Law of Human Performance, then quiz the scholars on the effective ways of studying. The results will indicate the understanding of the study skill and scholars will demonstrate how it is applied. A concern may be made that this would take away from class time.

In actuality, the Power Law of Human Performance will increase the speed and productivity of the scholars. Others may make the statement that devoting an entire class for studying cannot fit in the school hours. To that I would say, schools find time to put many different events in the schedule for the scholars. Such as field trips, movie day, sports, pep rallies, special assemblies, and board games. So, there is always enough time to learn how to study or redevelop study skills. The Power Law of Human Performance is a proven study technique to increase knowledge and create life-long learners.

To All Scholars:

Do not stop with just studying your course work, but study everything that pertains to you and your success. Study your University(ies) and staff. Study your Scholarships. Study your Major Curriculum(s). Study your Colleagues. Study your future companies for employment. Study your future business(es).

Resolve: Go ahead and decide "to decide to study" before you study. Prepare yourself to advance. It-is-Possible. You must decide not to be average or mediocre. Do not be scared to be great. It is already in you. There is nothing average about God. I am made in the image and likeness of God, our creator, and so are you.

Just to let you know. Decisions are made when you do not decide. Choosing to stand still when life is moving around you, will cause you to be left behind. Life has moved ahead of you while you are still indecisive. Not making your decision is a decision. By surrendering your decisions, you will be swept away in any direction. Make a conscious decision to learn and study for your success.

THE RIGHT **K.E.Y.** to Mastery is

Practicing.

Knowledge **E**difies **Y**ou to Mastery!

"Never regard study as a duty, but as the enviable opportunity to learn." Albert Einstein

"DECIDE to COMMIT to being a SCHOLAR!"

Chapter 4

T – TUITION COGNITION

"When you know your rights and values,

you have the ability and option to never be at a disadvantage."

If you are in a situation where you have been given a title deed or someone has left a gift for you that is paid in full, your response is critical.

You must search it out to know what it is: or you will never know the full value of what you possess. It is okay to **ask** questions about what you receive. It is not an indication of ungratefulness. It is an indication of your appreciation and interest in what you have been given.

"...the honor of kings is to search out a matter." Proverbs 25:2. Remember to A.S.K. – Ask, Seek and Knock! Matthew 7:7-8

There are six (6) main responses:

First, Be thankful.

Second, know exactly what you have.

Third, know the value.

Fourth, know when it is effective.

Fifth, know where it can be used.

Finally, know how to use it.

First, be thankful: In the words of my paternal grandmother, "Thank you makes room for more and more." Please **Be** Continually **Thankful, Be** Consistently **Grateful,** and Always **Appreciate** what people do and how people treat you. Whatever the amount, it is important to remember people are being kind to you. Therefore, being grateful and kind is how you want to respond. My dad asked a group of scholars a question. One student got the answer correct. My dad gave him a dollar. The student complained and said, "Is this all I get." My dad said, "Okay, wait a minute, give that one back." The young man gave my dad the dollar back and was expecting more from my dad, but my dad just took the dollar back. No matter what people are willing to give you, usually it has some value. It all depends on one's perception. People have options. Be thankful and appreciate all you are blessed to acquire. The truth is one dollar could have paid for something, even if it were for taxes or investing.

Second, *know exactly* **what you have**_:_ Is it a scholarship, voucher, gift, loan, grant, stipend, award, or allowance? Know what you have been given. I had to learn this lesson quickly. When you know what you have and you know your tuition amount, you may **ask** if there are other funds available? Just knowing you have something to help you through this journey is vital. If the proper information is not known, you will be at a disadvantage, because you do not have the knowledge of what you possess. Knowing the full extent of what you have and what you are paying for as you achieve your degree(s) is important.

Third, *know* **the value**_:_ How much is the award worth? I have learned it is important to know the amount of your scholarship, college tuition and how it is allocated. You need to know the value of what you have been given and if all expenses will be covered. Usually, the cash value of the fund is indicated. **Ask** for what is covered and ask for what is not covered in the scholarship. **Ask** for a list of all additional amenities and a list of necessary items needed or necessities for each course.

Fourth, *know **when** it is effective:* The question of "when" is urgent. The answers to when tells you,
- What Semester type? Spring only, fall, summer only, fall and spring only, may-mester, winter-mester, or one-time only.
- When is it Effective? Freshman year or sophomore year.
- What is the Duration? 4 years, 5 years or just 1 year; renewable; non-renewable and when you must re-apply.
- When will funds be Released? Pre-funds before the semester begins, after enrollment only, after courses begin, mid-semester, once per month or at the end of the semester.

Fifth, *know **where** it can be used:* Can your scholarship be applied to all majors or is it only for a particular college or department within the college? Will the scholarship follow me to any university? Is it only used at an Historically Black College or University (HBCU)? Is it a university aid or scholarship only?

Also, know where your tuition and fees are being allocated. You may have access to an abundance of university opportunities. I Know where my fees are going and make sure that I take advantage of all the opportunities presented to me to advance my career(s). Many fees are set in place and paid for by the scholars. Some scholars do not know how to take advantage of the opportunities that are available to them. To find these answers, simply ask questions.

Finally, how may I use it? If you have a scholarship, know what your scholarship covers or how you may use the funds. Your scholarship may have special benefits. Is the scholarship based on need only? Is it a merit scholarship?

Ask what your scholarships can do for you. If you do not know, you may miss out on a plethora of great things and events.

Ask how are the funds being used? Does it cover the entire tuition, room, board, books, technical tools, professional clothing allowance, educational travels: lodging and meals; transportation or a combination; a portion of each or only one of the areas mentioned?
By the way, what is board? Board in this text is food or meals. From the word, cupboard, or food cabinet. It is critical to know if your food is one meal per day, all meals for the entire week, all meals for the weekdays only or a limited number of meals altogether.

Ask if your tuition covers resume paper, career development workshops, are the funds linked to a certain organization and so much more. May I cash out the balance for other educational needs; will the funds be reimbursed; or will the purchase of my school materials be reimbursed (if so, partially, or fully reimbursed)? Will it limit me from applying for other funds or will it cause an automatic cancelation of other scholarships? May I use the funds for online materials for each level of my classification or are the materials automatically included in my tuition.

In the application process, ask if there is a way to reduce or minimize your fees. One question could cut down the cost of your college education or waive fees.

So, make sure as a college scholar you know exactly what those fees are going towards and what they do for you. Anything that your University offers that could help your career, you should absolutely take it. Knowledge is powerful. When you have this knowledge, you can apply for additional support, if needed.

With this knowledge you can better prepare yourself, help produce change, vote, and even direct difference.

At my university, a scholar may apply for all sorts of scholarships. Just **A.S.K.** questions.

Here are some scholarship opportunities...

1. LS-Lamp and Timbuktu (The best option with on-going support.)
2. Foundation Scholarships
3. Niche.com
4. Moolahspot.com
5. Scholarship.com
6. Mos.com (Great Option)

"Scholar A.S.K. questions. It is a gift of peace and a crown to kings!"

Chapter 5
R – RELENTLESS RESOURCES

"We stand on the shoulders of many who have been diligent, it will be time for others to stand on our shoulders.
Let's keep the legacy strong."

There are at least five types of resources. Resources can be natural like the sun and water. Revenue or wealth are forms of resources. Resources are viewed as materials and supplies. Knowledge gained through information is a resource. However, the most valuable resources are found in people.

People ask, why do I quote so many. Well, it is because all these people have impacted my life. They are a resource in some way *(and I expect more people to reach out and impact my life)*. Some of the great things people say to me are invaluable seeds of wisdom.

Like many others, I have heard the quote, "It takes a village to raise a child." This is true, but the question is, why is it important? Well, I believe the reason why it takes an entire village is because people who speak into our lives are actually sowing seeds. When the village helps one person, they are literally impacting a harvest of others. The reverberations from the powerful impact of words, and deeds is not only momentarily beneficial, but its effect is also multi-generational.

Wise people view things circumspectly and generationally. Initially, the founders of Southern University made a choice and resolution which appeared to only reach 12 scholars and 5 faculty members from a small geographical location. Over the decades and beyond the original members, an untold harvest has been affected, and empowered over multiple generations and nations. Today, the impact continues. Use your imagination to see the many families, communities and yes nations. People who have taken the time to teach us, given and share with us, need us to listen and learn so the knowledge and wisdom will not be lost.

Personally, there are people I quote that I have never met and those I hope to meet in the future. These people who have impacted my life speak through me each time I reach out to impact others. Their kind words of wisdom and knowledge grow up into a harvest so many others may learn. As my village increases, I am sure the greatest harvest of the seeds of wisdom and knowledge is yet to be revealed.

Remember, Pride has no place in knowledge. As people impact our lives, we will impact the lives of so many others. Ask questions and allow people to share in your life. As they help you, they are helping generations.

My Assigned Resources

I call people resources, My "Purpose People." The ones God has assigned to me. They do not want to hinder you. These are the ones who want to see you succeed and want to help you. Whenever they help you, they have literally helped themselves. Identify those people who are there to help you, not just your friends. Also, watch for supporters, the people who can really help your college career, your professional career, and your life. These people will let you know in their demeanor, they are for you and *not against you*. These are not just the people you hang around.

I have discovered these people to be in my family, friends, church family, professors, faculty, staff, colleagues, and people I have met through visiting different places. You may have the opportunity to witness the lives of these people up close.

I have two P.I.P. sisters. P.I.P. means, **P**ushing **I**mportant **P**eople. My sisters, Brianna and Brejena are Brilliant, Beautiful, and Business Entrepreneurs.

Brianna is my first P.I.P. I watch her resilience. She is so strong, extremely smart, and never gives up. She is married to Dennis and they have two children, Imani and Aulani. Brianna still helps me with her knowledge, understanding and experiences. In school, Brianna taught me Physics, Sciences, Mandarin Chinese, Vocabulary, Math, Physical Education, and English/Grammar.

My sister, Brejena, is exceptionally smart and humorous but does not tolerate people who want to hurt or hold others down. She is always working on making us better. Brejena creates health products to make people live and look healthier. In school, she taught me Business Marketing, English/Grammar, Music, Health, and Entrepreneurship. They are never stagnated and moving forward. (***Side note***: My sisters are not ready for my voice change. I am taller than both sisters.)

When I meet or learn of my "Purpose People," I instantly desire to be a blessing to them. And I know, one day God will help me fulfill this desire.

ELIJAH J. D. PRECCIELY

Everyone needs a *Ruth*, rather a "Mrs. Ruth!"

"Even the Best person who does not heed to the Influence from <u>Women of Wise Increase</u> is like the Finest Rolls Royce with NO Engine, Nor Interior!"

In the book of Ruth, Ruth provided Naomi with Strength, Guidance, Knowledge, Support, and so much more.

Some of my "Purpose People" are countless women who have an instrumental role in my life. I am not well versed on females, but according to the Bible and the evidence in my life, women are critically important.

Every man, young or old, who succeeds <u>as a leader,</u> there is a real godly woman who is giving <u>to</u> them with great honor. Sometimes they can be a mother, sister, niece, cousin, administrator, staff, professor....

These women represent the epitome and personification of strength, wisdom, compassion, order, prudence and are strong and dependable like a **R.O.C.K.**

1. With <u>Revelation</u>, they give a true understanding and expose wrong.
2. With <u>Order</u>, they operate as a Commander and optimize systems and processes.
3. With <u>Compassion</u>, they give support, corroboration, and use discretion to help correct flaws.
4. With <u>Keen Foresight</u>, they provide wisdom and clear prudence by operating as Prophetess (seers).

"Just follow their INSTRUCTIONS."

Be wise and learn from their wisdom, understanding, and knowledge.

I have met all these great successful women while they were helping others selflessly and succeeding themselves. The people just needed to follow their instructions.
These individuals R.O.C.K. in my life:

B.C. – Before and during College is my mother, my sisters, my cousin who is like-a-sister, Cache.
My personal Prophetess is Ms. Gail Bowie.
My personal Apostle is Mrs. Willetta Burks.
My Personal Praying in the Spirit Edifier is Sis. Stephanie Ellerson
My personal Evangelists are Sis. Bertha Rogers, Evangelist Barnia McKines, and Mrs. Yvonne Bey.

D.C. – During College:

Mrs. Bernice Ruth M.S. **Kind, Consistent, Organized, Unconditional, Prayer Warrior, Angel, Holistically Professional Advisor, Sees the outer person, and Sees and Checks on the heart**

Professor Tanganika Johnson M.S. (True College Scholar Led Educator, Protector and Preserver)

Mrs. Sharon Saunders M.S. (Administrative Advisor and Connector)

Professor Deadra Mackie M.S. (Professor, Academic, Research and Prudence Option Advisor)

Ms. Lashounda Franklin M.S. (Unending Opportunity Advisor)

Dr. Augusta Smith (Professor and Creative Solution Research Advisor)

Ms. Lynette Jones (Equipment Support and Career Follow-up)

Mrs. Elydia Poydras (Professional Business, Prayer and Ministry)

Mrs. Melissa Duff-Brown (Invention and Innovative Business Director)

Professor Marsha Robbins, M.S. (Initial Accommodating and Support Advisor)

Dr. Manicia Finch (Discerning Advisor)

Mrs. Deanna Smith (Camp C.E.E.S. Seer and Advancer)

Mrs. Tamara Montgomery (Career/Employer for Volunteerism)

Ms. Edy Davis (First RadioVision Broadcast Assistant)

My Gifted Professors in the order given to me by God *(You are so special to me. When I just think of you, I smile.)*:

Professor Amreen Ajaz, M.S.
Professor Phedra Wells, M.S.
Professor Tiffany Vappie, M.S.

Professor Kissie Anderson, M.S.
Professor Dr. Juanita Bates
Professor Dr. Karen Crosby
Professor Sylvia Olwochi M.S.

Professor Dr. Sharon Nicholas-Omoregbe
Professor Dr. Katrina Cunningham
Professor Brittany Lee M.S.
Professor Lauri Patterson M.S.

My Unique Administrators who bless me with unconditional kindness: *(Your consistency has blessed me tremendously.)* Alphabetical Order:

Mrs. Beatrice Armstrong
Mrs. Tracie Barton
Mrs. Beulah Lavergne-Brown
Mrs. Chrisena Williams-Brown

Mrs. Jennifer Caldero, M.S.
Mrs. Avis O. Chaney M.S.
Mrs. Christina Crump
Mrs. Dianna Gilbert-Depron

Dr. Rachel Vincent-Finley
Mrs. Heather Freeman
Mrs. Marva Hawkins
Mrs. Kathy Hayes

Mrs. Patricia Hebert
Mrs. Whitney Jones-Holland
Ms. Toni Jackson M.S.
Dr. Maryam Jahan

Dr. Lena Johnson
Mrs. Valerie P. Jones
Mrs. Dawn Kight (and All the Librarian Faculty)
Mrs. Brenda McNeely

Mrs. Donna Rogers
Dr. Joyce O'Rourke
Mrs. Jenifer Peters

Mrs. Kathy Scott
Dr. Kimberly Ferguson-Scott
Mrs. Rosemary Sims

Dr. Akai Smith
Mrs. Janene Tate
Mrs. Rosey Taylor
Mrs. Paula Turner

> **To *ALL* the women who help keep our university beautiful and To *ALL* those who make sure I eat right in the Union, Pod, and the Cafe. Thank YOU!**

These women love to learn and stay up on new technology. They greet me with goodness.

They are consistent (keep up with me) and will not slight me on information and knowledge.

When I want to make a difference, they will not despise or be despondent. I am confident there are many more unmentioned and many more who will increase in my life.

By the end of the Book of Ruth, she received her blessings, restoration, and increase (by relationship, wealth, and posterity).

I speak much respect, restoration, increase and blessings to be fulfilled in their lives in the way they have blessed me.

ELIJAH J. D. PRECCIELY

To all the women who **R.O.C.K.** in my life,

My Fully Packaged Resources

One thing is for sure, college is a place to develop your skills to research and develop all areas of resources. Remember God is our source, our power. When you know your source, you create a connection of perpetual potential to function effectively. You bring solutions even in untoward and problematic situations. You may not think of everything, but you can be the catalyst, incentive, or inspiration to ignite ideas within others.

In addition to knowing resources around you are vital, knowing what YOU offer and what resources you possess is K.E.Y. We have been given everything that pertains to life and godliness. In other words, we have everything we need in us to create the best world around us.

We must identify and appreciate the gifts that are in each of us to help one another, unity. A present, with so much value. WE are fully equipped and packaged. When given the space to use our voices together, others will see we are not just the future, we are the present as well. There is no need to copy, be jealous or envious of anyone else.

I am unequivocally different and being different makes me even more valuable. Each of us must discover and understand our differences and use all our potential to work together to make a difference in the lives of others in a blessed way.

My Diverse Resources

Starting college full time, some would think because of my age, I could only embrace certain people. However, at my university, Southern University and Agricultural & Mechanical College located in Baton Rouge, Louisiana, I have met people from all over the world.

My entire university is a classroom for learning, in itself. When I speak with people from different and diverse backgrounds, I learn what their life is like; or hear about their stories; and what brought them here or back here. I gain much knowledge. Seeing first-hand how esteemed people are from many walks of life is a respected honor.

Some people only mention discrimination based on race, religion, gender – but they should also include age, profession, country, accent, or dialect. My university is completely diverse, and I am proof. The faculty, staff and my colleagues embrace me.

My colleagues are resourceful and do not mind sharing their knowledge. Knowledge is here to help us all. Because there are many people on campus, it may seem like you will not fit in or standout. However, just know at Southern University, you are important; you are noticed; and you are a valuable resource. What you contribute is priceless.

As you consider the types of resources you have in people, keep in mind to let others help you.

The truth is, when it comes to learning, we all need each other. The right knowledge is like the right music, it is a universal language that teaches us healing, deliverance and how to learn from our past so we can all move forward in our present and future. Knowledge teaches us the melody of kindness. Scholars,...

Don't Be "Ruth-less!!!"

"Because Even the Strongest Bricks need Mortar to Stand."

Chapter 6

U – UNDERSTANDING UNLIMITED

"Projecting is a big problem. It indicates your perspective but undermines the capabilities of others."

When it comes to knowledge and innovations, many people think things are hard, impossible, and abstruse. But it is their own thoughts, views and abased experiences being subconsciously (or consciously) projected towards others.

Understanding One Another:

Just because something is difficult for one, does not mean it will be difficult for everyone else. WE should not judge or generalize people in this fashion. We should speak life to ourselves and others. Encourage others and let them know they can accomplish it.

Everyone is different. Personally, I thoroughly enjoy all subjects. Knowledge and information are interesting to me. It is and will always be interesting. This is the way God has made me and I am confident in who I am. I respect when others have challenges, but it does not mean they will not succeed. We must be patient with one another.

My purpose is different from anyone else. It is like food. Some people enjoy coconuts, others have an allergic reaction; and some just do not like to eat coconuts. This is the same way with various subjects. Some people will enjoy a particular field of study; some will have an uncomfortable reaction to it; others just do not prefer and cannot tolerate the field of study. I am okay with this. It is important not to project your experiences on others.

Just because a person does not know a particular subject "YET", does not mean they will not learn it. It may only take a new teacher or someone to show them in a different way.

We must be patient with one another. We should understand and realize, even though an area may have been arduous for a group of people, does not mean it is hard for everyone. There are always exceptions. Both, Discouragement and Encouragement are like sonic boom waves transferring vibrational energy; the sound resonates to a long distance away. Speak good things over yourself and others despite your previous experiences. Even though you experienced the worst, you must encourage and help others to advance. Wish people the best!

Understanding our Professors:

Be the type of person who understands the big picture and how professors contribute. Our professors have devoted their lives to a subject matter. Do not be the person to treat professors or the course you are studying for your degree, carelessly. Your professor has great value. Great professors want you to succeed. They committed themselves to support your interest, even if it is different from theirs. They are of great value to us.

When I find a **professor**, who loves to speak with me about their field of expertise, I am overjoyed and tremendously intrigued. I can and have spoken with professors for extensive lengths of time about subject matter and valuable knowledge, especially Professor Kissie Anderson, Dr. D. Bagayoko, Dr. Juanita Bates, Dr. Katrina Cunningham, Professor and Coach Geralds, Dr. King David Godwin, Dr. Laurence Henry, Professor Tanganika Johnson, Professor Deadra Mackie, Dr. Eduardo Martinez, Mr. Jason Ordogne,

Professor Sherman Pitman, Dr. Augusta Smith, Dr. Anthony Stewart, and Dr. R. C. Walker *(Professors, thank you for sharing and allowing me to have so much of your time. I hope you did not mind, and I pray you will be available for more valuable conversations.)* When you accept the fact that your professor is a person, you get to see how much they really want you to succeed.

In addition, your professors and administrators have the authority to write you an acceptable letter of recommendation.

Do not make the mistake of others who began college as a freshman and presented themselves as if they do not care. When, in their senior year decide to look and act like a professional in attitude, language, appearance, and behavior. This will not go over well with the professor. Not many professors are willing to put their name on the line for such students. It is time to get serious and conduct yourself as <u>First-Class</u> before you go to your <u>First Class</u>. I spoke with a professor who said, "You have to look and conduct yourself so I can write a letter of recommendation."

>Here is a ==Gold Brick==: Be wise and do not create a presentation or create a document that would keep you from receiving a letter of recommendation from a professor. To receive a professional letter of recommendation you must have professional conduct. Professors can see what you are really like from your repeated decisions and behavior. ==*"Scholar, KNOW your True Value and the Wealth of your God given Vision; and do not Compromise Standards!"*==

Chapter 7

C – CHEATING EXTIRPATES

"People Cheat when they do not try and when they do not try, they cheat themselves out of opportunities to do great things."

Mahatma Gandhi said, *"Satisfaction lies in the effort, not in the attainment, full effort is full victory."* Because of my purpose, I have spoken to many and I will travel and speak around the world. I have noticed a lack of hope from elementary school to college. People need to be encouraged to believe the impossible can be possible.

I want others to have the necessary K.E.Y.s to learn for life. It is okay not to know everything, but it is not okay to rob yourself of the opportunity. Take in the knowledge, learn it, and be prepared to apply it. Opportunities come with challenges. Nevertheless, we need everyone on board to accept the opportunities to change our world for the better.

Many people do not realize how connected we are. We are all like a grid. We are connected in some way or another. My integrity affects others and vice versa. Doing what is right creates the right impact. We should all be rectitudinous and honest in our character without being piously self-righteous.

Integrity in your school

When a person cheats, they lie to themselves and justify their decision with excuses. Make sure you are not a person of excuses using disparaging and hopeless statements such as "It is better to cheat than repeat; this class does not matter in the real world; or No one cares if I pass or fail." There is absolutely no excuse for the lack of integrity. It is just pushing things off to mount up for a greater demise. Be responsible inch by inch. As the Bible says, little by little.

Always remember this K.E.Y., cheating is a lack of integrity. First, do not allow yourself to believe the lie that all students cheat. Scholars do not cheat. Since you are a Scholar, you do not cheat either. Secondly, a lack of integrity does not stop in just one area. It spreads like a virus. Cheating in elementary school or in your college career is not good. It inhibits the ability to learn and potentially impedes functioning in your business and the corporate world.

Integrity in your Business

Cheating makes people unprepared for life. It will also damage credibility even if the person does not get caught. For example, if a person owns their business, a lack of integrity or cheating will impact their business decisions to cut corners, be inconsistent or lower standards. A decrease in standards reduces customer confidence in any product or service which will affect profits in any industry.

Integrity in your Corporate Career

Cheating reduces confidence which breeds insecurities. When you have the opportunity to be in an interview, the representative can tell if you know what you are talking about. When I interview individuals, I can tell if they are free to dialog about what is on their resume. A clear conscience is an aura! If people cheat, they inhibit their mental growth and harm their ability to learn new things. It is not good for the brain. **Lying actually decreases the density of grey matter in the spinal cord which affects the nervous system, and its consequences extend throughout the entire body as well as damages cognitive functions** [8].

Imbalance of Integrity

A lack of integrity in one area is a lack of integrity in other areas. Academic grades and social skills have their place, but if you do not have good character to match, you still have an imbalance of understanding and knowledge. At Southern University, our Professors are not only concerned about our academics, but they also want us to grasp, understand and succeed in life. Professors are simply affirming you have learning. They have many options, whether by test, demonstration, research, or presentation, it is to affirm. While, I have gained good character examples during my course study with all my professors. I remember a particular lesson learned about using integrity and respectability when interacting with others from Professor P. Wells' class. A student entered the classroom with an unusual smell. Professor Wells noticed the student, but she did not mortify him. She was discreet towards him and took time to teach all of us firm standards and instructions on how to come to class and better ourselves. We cannot present or conduct ourselves in just any manner. There are standards. What we do influences, motivates, and has an effect on those around us. Our professors are developing and increasing our scholars to possess good character without partiality. Character will not only get you the job, business, and career, but character will keep, increase, and open more doors within the opportunities.

It is great to lead with integrity. As the usage of technology expands and increases, companies will considerably intensify their search for people with integrity. They are looking for those who can be trusted with opportunities to have an enormous impact. Businesses want results whether in person or offsite from the office without having someone to look over their shoulders. For some, doing what is right may not always be easy, but it is worth it.

Just Remember, some opportunities may come with challenges. If there is a difficulty look for the opportunity. Albert Einstein said,

"In the middle of every difficulty lies opportunity."

My dad preached a message about Samson. It was after Samson killed a lion with his bare hands. Samson created a riddle for his Philistine guest. It is found in Judges 14:14, "Out of the eater, something to eat; out of the strong, something sweet." In your life there are situations you may have to conquer, but understand you are the winner. Do what is right for the present because it is directly connected to your future. You must make the decision to focus on the circumstances or see the blessing. My dad said it best for situations and people,

"Look for the Honey."

Keep the whole **P. I. E.** Standards and you will do well!

P – Professionalism

I – Integrity

E – Ethics

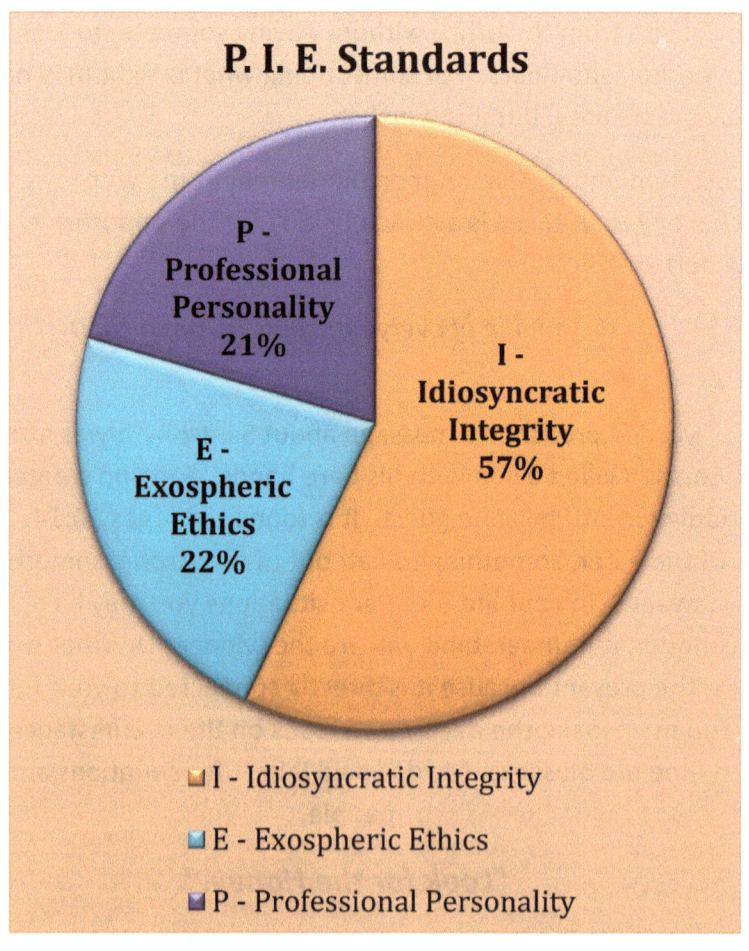

ELIJAH J. D. PRECCIELY

"People Cheat when they do not believe in themselves and when they do not believe in themselves, they do not try."

"Scholar, begin each day, class, and task with I Believe I can!"

Chapter 8

T – TECHNOLOGY TRANSCENDS TIME

"The prohibitors of technology are those who refuse to advance the present."

As people begin to embrace technology for its infinite possibilities in the classroom, there will be an increase in learning due to virtual knowledge. Pay close attention to how technology is used more and more in the classroom and especially at home. This means scholars are beginning to learn at a more rapid pace when it is presented correctly.

> *"Technology won't replace teachers...But teachers who use technology will probably replace teachers who do not."*
> *Dr. Ray Clifford*

Today, neither cybersecurity, safety nor laws have truly advanced with our growing technology. Our world has advanced at a rapid rate where science, technology, engineering, and math are used in every aspect of our lives. STEM usage will continue at an accelerated rate. We must surge forward above the technology. It is imperative for me to be more educated with academic advancements, holistic research, and community influence.

Initially, I had to realize I entered my college studies with one of the most unique situations (opportunities). Although I am younger than most, I enjoy conducting many hours of independent study. Since I entered my course study with great and highly knowledgeable professors, my world of academic advancement has increased even more. I want to make sure this never stops. When independent knowledge meets corporate knowledge, there is revelation and innovation. This is what I experience everyday while studying here at Southern University and Agricultural & Mechanical College.

When theory meets practicum, we form an unbreakable bridge of knowledge. I have a great understanding of theory and personal research, which has provided me with amazing futuristic ideas and inventions. I was informed that my university of choice was only a teaching university, but since I have entered college full time, I have found a Holistic Research environment. My personal research and theoretical knowledge are being confirmed through research studies with published professors such as Dr. A. Stewart (Physics and Engineering); Dr. E. Martinez (Biology); Dr. A. Smith (Biology); Dr. R.C. Walker (Agriculture); and Dr. M. Zhao (Physics and Mathematics). Just communicating with educators who understand my language is incredible and fulfilling. This must continue!

As I advance in my studies and research, I always remember a quote by my Mom, "Son, knowledge hidden is unfruitful, but knowledge shared is a seed for an abundant harvest." When I share my knowledge and wisdom with scholars and young people around the world, I am giving back for a greater harvest. With the prestigious opportunity to influence my generation, I want to pave the way for others to enter the world of being life-long learners, Scholars. I know that we all must do our part to inspire the world, but I have moved from inspiration to impact. I cannot stop!

Since, I have been full-time at the age of 11 years old, my studies in Physics and Mechanical Engineering have been remarkable. This decision has further afforded me the opportunity to continue my academic advancements, engage in intriguing research and community influence from inspire to impact. Advancing our world with knowledge and innovations for a better, safer, quality living is everyone's business.

Scholar, know the value of your tools!

While growing up, my dad had a brother, they called Lee Lee (Uncle Lee Lee to me). He was the brother a few years older than my dad. During **Y**oung **P**eople **W**illing **W**orker (Y.P.W.W.) Service at their church, sometimes the youth would play a game called Bible Drill. The participants would hold the closed Bible in their hand and when the conductor would call out the Bible verse. The team members would have to locate the Bible Book, Chapter, Verse and quickly read it out loud.

Needless to say, my dad and Uncle Lee Lee would win many times. This type of game allowed my dad and other youth to learn to use their tool, which is the Bible. I have played this game. It is wonderful. The K.E.Y. is the tool. Knowing how to accomplish a task manually has its place for historical information but knowing how to swiftly produce using technical tools is greater. Accessibility, familiarity, and perfecting usage with up-to-date and advanced tools is the comparative advantage that rules. We must learn speed and accuracy with our technology.

I have some ideas for technology and approaches for learning. There are at least eight main ways scholars can use technology while learning. If you are a parent or scholar, you should learn and prepare for these proofs.

1. **Proof of Technology Tools:** Research Based Learning – Since the internet is truly vast, you can find any information you please. Therefore, scholars should be able to use their personal devices to investigate subject matter. As well as use the internet to search out learning resources and tools needed for quizzes and tests. Scholars are finding information and increasing their ability to retain knowledge by being allowed to investigate subject matter and concepts for themselves before and/or during class period. ***On the Spot Research*** can be used to develop accuracy of knowledge and speed with tools associated with real knowledge. To make things more efficient for use; there can be a campus wide block on the Wi-Fi for certain websites. This will eliminate incorrect information and inappropriate usage while in the classroom.
Special Tip: Each home should be required to have family support, edible food, clean running water, safe electricity, cool air, warm heat, stable internet, and up-to-date computers. These are the new essential tools for developing and equipping minds for effective learning. The lack or decline of any of these is a disruption of stable and progressive learning.
2. **Proof of Increased Integrity:** The new purpose of testing is gathering accurate data. Using personal or mobile devices eliminates the concern for cheating. Tests given online should be used to track accurate searches (sources) of information or track if the scholar used incorrect sites for gathering data. Gathering or researching information

during tests using simulated scenarios for instant application is more favorable. Using electronic devices to verify the ability to research and maneuver information to complete tasks and produce results is needed in business and the corporate world.

No class time missed. With login and time tracking, even if the scholar was sick during class time, they can participate in the class lesson and assignments along with the professor. Each question assignment can be evaluated in real-time with the option to resolve any errors, immediately. This also reduces teacher task stress.

If all universities take a page out of homeschool, educators will be in the active role of an Educator Facilitator. The Educator will facilitate learning by guiding, directing with non-micro-managing. This is creating life-long learners and affirming knowledge. Basic information is independently researched, then additional knowledge is given by the educator. The information confirmed and updated by the scholar.

3. **Proof of updated Devices:** Maybe a harsh reality for some, but ALL scholars should be given; have access in class; or home to the MOST up-to-date tool/device. During registration, the scholar must enter the device to verify if there is a need for an upgrade or a new device needs to be purchased. In the words of Emmert Wolf, "A man is only as good as his tools." In my world, we should not only have the best tools, but also the best practice with the tools to <u>gain understanding, accuracy then speed</u> to **produce and create.**

4. **Proof of Usage:** Primary Schools are wasting money when the phones and electronic devices are not being used. The most up-to-date phones can be used as educational tools. A larger capacity device is only needed for better handling, computer drawing, Computer Aided Design (CAD), typing accessibility and for presentations or drawings. Each presentation can be like a Tedtalk.

5. **Proof of Knowledge:** All of our scholars have been trained to be evaluated by paper, but this is a slow thinking process. The automation testing or Socratic method of testing will allow scholars to present their mid-term and/or final with on-the-spot results. Even the math can be worked out and submitted on the screen with instant response. Memorizing formulas are over. Researching and learning the best formula to use and demonstrating how to use them is the norm based on the scenario. Being resourceful is the K.E.Y.: Searching out the best formulas, manipulating formulas, and applying them to solutions. The strategy is knowing the Order of Instructions, (Rules and Steps). Knowledge can no longer be abstract; learning is conducted like a job with all your resources available for your retrieval. You must follow the instructions and know how to access and use your tools.

6. **Proof of Understanding:** Scholars will no longer take tests on paper. Why? Because some students are just good test takers, but not producers with understanding and knowledge. This is fruitless. Education must return to producing. All paper tests should cease. Real life scenarios will be administered through technology using

the Socratic Method. Imagine focusing on one question per screen and seeing illustrations to assist with understanding. The scholar will openly answer questions while thoroughly explaining solutions and demonstrate using K.E.Y. words and procedures for evaluations. We have the capability to create life-long learners to change our world for the better with technology.

7. **Proof of Listening:** Making scholars write while they should be listening is antiquated. The K.E.Y. word is "Give your Full Attention." Scholars will be able to fully engage in knowledge. Scholars will manipulate given images or use their imagination to develop an image from the concepts being taught. The goal is to ensure concepts are being conveyed and understood.

8. **Proof of Advancement:** With more progressions in technology, professors are given the privilege of being abreast and advanced in the applications. To verify how concepts work, scholars and professors will be directly connected online with corporate professionals in their field. Professors and scholars will maintain active degrees by applying theory and practicum with real-time knowledge and applications.

"If we teach today as we were taught yesterday, we rob our children of their tomorrow." *John Dewey*

"Scholar, We must remember to make learning better for those who follow us!"

Chapter 9
I - INITIATE TO IGNITE CHANGE
and DO NOT STOP!

"The best thing a person can do for themselves and everyone around is to go to college and... finish to completion."

Left to Right: My Great Physics Professor and Advisor, Dr. A. Stewart and I during the annual Southern University and Agriculture & Mechanical College Science, Technology, Engineering, and Math (S.T.E.M.) Day

"You can initiate change in the world for the better with the right College Knowledge."

One of the biggest lies I have heard from those who finish college and those who never go to college is, *College is a waste of time* or *College is not for everyone."* Wow! Whoever believes this fake knowledge, is drastically deceived. The truth is knowledge is never, ever, never, ever wasted <u>on the wise</u> and a fool can learn to become wise with the right decisions.

Rule #1: To get rid of a fool, simply read and share knowledge out loud. *"The fear of the Lord is the beginning of knowledge, but fools despise wisdom and instruction."* Proverbs 1:7

Rule #2: To gain the right friends, watch their response to instructions, an increase in learning or wisdom in decisions. *"Give instruction to a wise man, and he will be yet wiser: teach a just man, and he will increase in learning."* Proverbs 9:9

Knowledge shifts the atmosphere, elevates minds and quiets or dismisses unruly situations and folly. Contrary to ignorance, when you attend College for knowledge, it is not just something to get away to do or just an experience. College is your Entrepreneurship Career! I am increasing knowledge, building wealth, and expanding networks. College is for knowledge, so the right College Knowledge can be powerful. We must re-establish the standards in education.

These are four of my starting K.E.Y.s I want you to know and understand to initiate change through attending college. The Plan, Purpose, Position and Profit for knowledge, then REPEAT! I must admit, I received my starting K.E.Y.s early, but these will get you ready. Keep it simple but think Big!

> **The Plan** *(What is my overall vision?)*:
> The Plan is to become…
>
> **The Purpose** *(What will this accomplish or fulfill?)*:
> I will be able to …
>
> **The Power** in Position *(What is my impact?)*:
> I will make a difference…
>
> **The Profit** *(What do I expect to manifest?)*:
> I will gain and increase…

There was a time in our history when people could not read, write, or go to school. Now, this is a time in our history where some people are disinterested or dropping out of school. The problem is those people are not connecting the dots to determine, "Why college?" They have taken on someone else's reasoning or negative ideas. You need to see how life advancements are connected to knowledge.

First, you must have **The Plan**. Not a plan or any plan, but the right plan. Not just what you *think* is the best plan or not just the easy plan. The best plan that yields the best results. Listen, your plan must include your major(s), college timeline, internship experience, your continued education, and career path. My areas of interest are vast in number and depth, I had to narrow my major down to two areas at this time: Physics and Mechanical Engineering. I like to discover how things work and then I like to create or improve things; and make them operate efficiently. However, I keep myself abreast in all areas of interest from all sciences and research to business, history, and theatre production. So, God can use me anywhere. I want to continue to be used by God.

"Legacy takes Preparation."

The Purpose is the reason why you want to conquer this area of study. Why are you interested in these areas? As I mentioned, I enjoy Physics and Mechanical Engineering because these areas allow me the good fortune of knowing how and why things operate. Then, I get to learn how to create or improve things more efficiently. Your reason for why you choose your area of interest may vary, but whatever your reason, keep it before you.

Southern University and Agricultural & Mechanical College is so great because I get to study all areas of interest. A K.E.Y.: I believe God has given me all these areas of interest for a divine purpose. But we must all have a starting point. So, select your major(s) wisely. Consider studying areas you may have been interested in as a child. Do not block your brain by making choices based on whether it is hard or easy. Ask God for grace, favor, and mercy. The plan is to make a better difference with all God has given you. Remember, only sometimes a career test may help, but the test may not reflect all you are designed to accomplish. Do not rely on the test alone. Also, make yourself acquainted with former graduates, professionals, and especially professors in your field of study. Your professors are real people. They have studied their entire lives to perfect their area of interest and to support their families; therefore, respect them and the courses they teach.

As you move forward towards graduation, your purpose will keep you focused so you will learn beyond your degree. Just because you graduate does not mean you should stop learning.

Each Position you will attain as a result of attending college is important. Your knowledge gained will place you in positions to help impact the lives of others and make decisions on their behalf. It starts with knowledge. Since I have been attending college, I have been placed in positions to help others become life-long learners, Scholars. I take every option to help initiate a spark to inspire and impact change for better lives. As a result of embracing knowledge, my learning experiences are endless. I am in the position to impact the lives of others in a great way. Just imagine if more people become creators rather than consumers only. People who are spectators should become participators of change. People who could not feed their families; in abusive situations are given the real lasting help they need to have a better life. This is because we acquired knowledge for ourselves and to help others. The solutions we have all been waiting for is amid the knowledge we acquire. Never Stop Learning, it will save lives.

Expecting to Profit from college as you acquire your degree is powerful. College is more than just taking classes to get a grade. I expect to increase my knowledge and apply it. I keep this portion of my vision before me each semester, each year and especially each summer. For each semester and summer, I knew I wanted to advance in research opportunities with Southern University. I want to interact with other people my age to encourage them to leap into S.T.E.M. (Science, Technology, Engineering, and Mathematics) especially Physics. I also want to participate in an abbreviated research internship with a corporation. I expected to do research, technology, and development.

> *"While acquiring knowledge, there is no time lost or wasted, if you DO NOT STOP."*
> *Dr. Jamar Montgomery, Esq.*

As you can see by the picture, I was able to reach my goal during my college career and participate in research projects and presentations in Physics and Chemistry; Physics and Engineering; Biology: and more: *Nitrated Cellulose in the

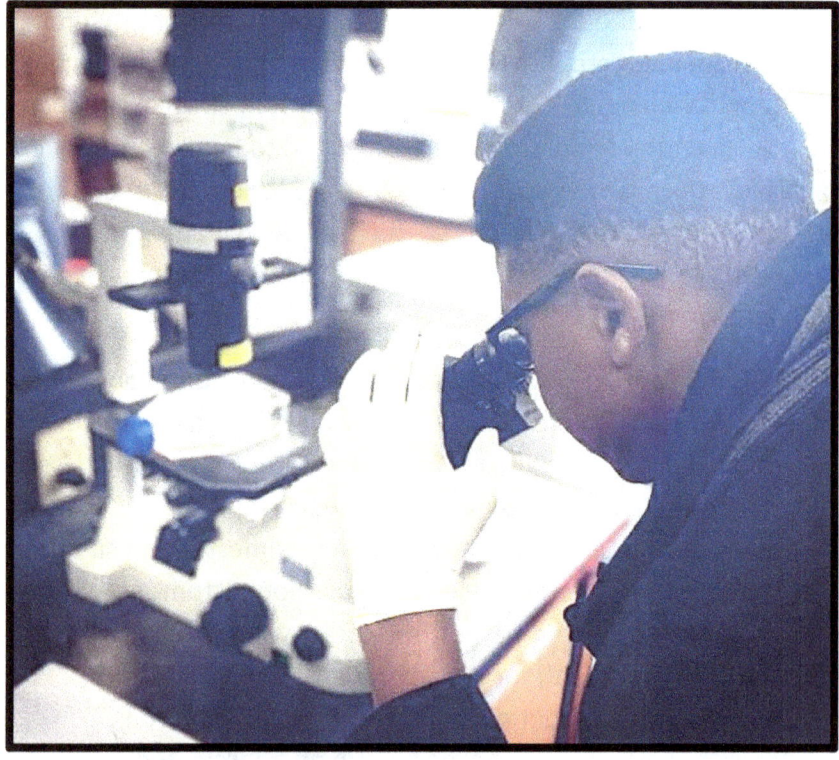

Production of Graphene; *Gene editing with HoxA1 gene to create knockout mice; *Effects of Magnets on Diverse Materials; *Quantum Ethics and Effects; *Unmanned Aerial Vehicle Development and Testing; *Graphene: The World's New Metal; *The Effects of Computer Games Versus Board Games. I expect to do development in several areas.

> *"When theory meets practicum, we form an unbreakable bridge of knowledge."*

My top advice to each scholar is before you begin college, get connected with Southern University's Career Service

Team, under the direction of Mrs. Tamara Montgomery as soon as you receive your acceptance letter. They are awesome! Some options to advance your career are study abroad, internships and research before graduating. I know internships may be available during your first semester and at least by the end of your second semester. Never leave college without an internship whether it is volunteer, non-paid or paid internship. Try your best to get the career experience with a local business, corporation or on campus. Ask for a letter of recommendation for your records.

    And I Repeat...What? If you stop learning, your degree is outdated. Keep reading and be sure to study new innovations. Once you get started it is not hard to continue. Remember Newton's 1st law of motion and Do not stop. The relevant reality is application. If a person does not apply what they have learned, this can be stagnating. However, knowledge can be stored until it is time to use it. It is okay to be the best you can be in college. Look for the best in yourself. As students and scholars, we are the reason why all the professors, administrator, staff, and faculty members are there. When you take a closer look, even the companies want to see us succeed. Each semester, I have met with representatives from NASA, Boeing, Lockheed Martin, etc. that literally take the time to answer questions I may present to them.

    It is K.E.Y. for us to understand how important we are. And how much our university wants to help us succeed, when we initiate change in the correct manners. The ultimate ==Gold Brick== lesson: Keep it going. It is better to keep something going rather than to stop it and try to start again. When you start again, settle in your heart and mind, "I Do Not Stop, My increase of Knowledge." In science, this is called Newton's 1st law of motion. A Body in motion will stay in motion, but a body at rest will stay at rest. It is easier to keep something great going rather than taking the effort to restart it. Never stop doing what is right. **Stick with it!**

My College Career Challenge for some of you:

1) The first step is in *your imagination*.
2) See yourself starting or returning to College.
3) See yourself interacting with your professors and other colleagues.
4) Begin filling out applications.
5) Get into education; Get back into education.
6) Be a finisher!
7) NEVER stop learning.
8) Share your success with the scholars around you.

If you would like, write me a letter of when you begin your courses, (and before each semester), a Letter when you finish, and the new opportunities you achieved! My email address is Aprodigy118@gmail.com My request to you is, take as many computer classes as you can and major or minor in STEM-E (Science (Physics), Technology, Engineering, Math, and Economics). Thanks!

EVERYONE SHOULD START COLLEGE, FINISH COLLEGE AND CONTINUE LEARNING.

"SCHOLAR, YOU ARE A FINISHER, I KNOW YOU CAN DO IT!"

Chapter 10
O – OPPORTUNITIES ARE OPTIONS

"Opportunities are like a two-edged sword; We must learn to receive as well as learn to give opportunities!"

There are numerous opportunities to succeed during your college career. Since I became a full-time college scholar at Southern University, I have found doors of opportunities from corporate internships and research to leadership.

There are many ways you can make opportunities count. Just begin with actively applying for scholarships, volunteering, internships (paid or unpaid), masters and doctoral programs, and research. During the semester and especially the career fair weeks, companies travel from far and near to hire our scholars.

I have been able to do some extraordinary things. Each semester, I refuse to miss the Southern University career fair. There are numerous companies who are not just attending, they participate to hire you. This great networking opportunity is grand. The consistency of the people from the companies is valuable. I appreciate when I attend the career fair and how some of the corporate people recognize me. You may ask, Why? Well, it is because I make sure I re-introduce myself to them. I am literally building relationships.

Although, I may not be old enough to work at some of these corporations; however, I am old enough to know the value of who they are and what they represent. For me, there are more than just internship opportunities to pursue. I have contacted companies like Lockheed Martin, Entergy, Procter & Gamble, Exxon Mobil, and many others. I believe all the companies would hire me, but the only reason why they do not is because I am only 12 years old.

Now, the Career Opportunities through the career services are exceptional. As a result of volunteering, I know from experience the great extent taken to bring serious opportunities to our scholars.

With so many opportunities, how does one decide... The opportunities through LS-Lamp (Louis Stokes – Louisiana Alliance for Minority Participation) are almost daily. The organization on campus is headed by Ms. L. Franklin and Dr. T. Reese (They are great!). LS-LAMP was established on our campus by Dr. D. Bagayoko.

Wow, I need help just sorting through the opportunities. The opportunities are strategic during your college career and into graduate and doctoral schools. "But wait, that is not All," you also receive a yearly scholarship for participating in weekly workshops. Representatives from around the world meet with us and provide opportunities. Listen, when we do what is asked of us, meaning – Following Instructions - THIS is wealth that accompanies wisdom.

No one should be afraid of the opportunities to do great things.

Optimum strategy for
The RIGHT K.E.Y. (Knowledge Edifies You) Advantage...

DO NOT WAIT, HESITATE, OR DELAY.

YOU MUST:

<mark>1) Ask about resources for Graduate School,</mark>

And

<mark>2) Ask about resources for Doctoral Programs.</mark>

There is so much available for scholars. You do not want to be the person who misses the opportunity of a lifetime. You do not want to be indecisive by not asking the right questions and accessing the right answers.

"P.O.O.R. stands for **Passed Over Opportunities Repeatedly**."

I learned this quote from my parents, who learned this from Apostle Louis Greenup. Do not pass up opportunities. Set a day aside or at least an evening each week to focus on filling out applications, writing essays and updating documents for opportunities. You can even call it O.P.P. Day (Opportunity Planning for Prosperity) or O.P.P. Night. O.P.P. for optimization. Just be consistent and stay on top of the dates.

In the words of Professor Kissie Anderson, who teaches so you love math, while balancing a trigonometric equation would say, *"Don't be stingy."* With all the opportunities we are privileged to be a part of, we must absolutely remember to create, share, provide, grant, and impart opportunities for others. We must not hold on to blessings just for ourselves. It will become like the excess manna the children of Israel tried to hold on to in the wilderness. The manna turned into maggots in their own tents. It did not just ruin some, it spoiled everything.

I have learned and confirmed: Take every opportunity to help improve or impact someone's life, Just Do It! Your harvest reward from your seed sown will always be greater, multiplied, expanded, and increased.

Scholar, The moral strategy of life's opportunities is,

"Don't Be Stingy."

Professor Kissie Anderson

Chapter 11
N – NOT READY? THINK AGAIN!

"To be Ready, it takes a decision and a state of mind."

To say college is not for everyone, is to say knowledge is not for everyone. Particularly, when we all benefit from the ongoing increase of knowledge around the world. Knowledge will allow us to advance, improve and even correct wrongs. We must continue to increase.

What is certain, College is not a place to get in debt; to get away from parents; or use student loans to party. College scholars should lead an abstemious lifestyle.

Make the Right Decisions:

One thing I can say for sure, people attend college for more than just to kick-start their career. Yes, I heard it too, "College is not for everyone." This is both a true and false statement. College is for everyone because it is a time to increase and research learning at a higher level. Everyone should attend and finish college. College is an atmosphere of knowledge. I understand parents are hopeful that college is a place of transition from immaturity to maturity; however, everyone is not ready to attain what college has to offer.

The fact is some young adults lack maturity. There are some students who attend college just to escape from their parents. Some expect to party from day one and assume all others are here to do the same with **very little to no** studying. Well, you do not have to attend college to get a loan to get away from parents to party. Just get a party loan. Focus on mastering how to live with roommates and be a part of the "HAC Life - Hang Around College life." This is such a waste of funds; however, it is true.

College is about decisions. It is the ability to independently make the right decision with multiple opportunities. Each day, I make a choice for class, assignments, projects, presentations, research, study abroad, internships and scholarships. Making right decisions now will protect and provide for me in my present and in my future.

Connect with Standards:

Your circle of people prophecies your future. Do not hang around with people whose speech portrays "nothing." Your speech will portray who you really are. Dr. Mike Murdock, "Show me your friends, and I will tell you your present and your future." Connect with people who take you out of your comfort zone(s), while sharpening your intellect. Do not be friends with haters. I have found that even though I am younger than my colleagues, I prefer to be in the company of those who are seriously interested in creating, research and development. I have a proposal and a plan. In the words of Dr. Cindy Trimm, "Those who have no plan are there to strip you of yours, because misery still loves company." These are people who get more excited when they hear when people are experiencing a tragedy, so they will feel better about themselves or have someone and something to talk about. Your network will either create or destroy opportunities, so network with wisdom first.

> "Knowledge untold and withheld is a crime to the world."

Believe Again:

People do not believe the impossible can be possible. I am proof as an example to show you, the impossible is possible. You must have the God kind of faith. Most do not know how to think outside the box or to think big. They have lost hope.

But Think Again:

Doctors try your Research *Again*

Preachers try that message *Again*

Comedians try that joke *Again*

Professors teach scholars *Again*

Planners try that Strategy *Again*

Dreamers and Visionaries see *Again*

Scholars learn *Again*

Former scholars come back to school *Again* and complete your vision!

In other words, ***imagine Again***. All things are possible to those who **just believe**.

Finally,

> *Do not take on the nature of the things or people that hurt or harm you,*
> *1) acknowledge the painful wrong,*
> *2) decide to learn and grow from it,*
> *3) understand it is not about you, and*
> *4) help others to avoid and heal from the hurt!*

Have you heard of the Spirit of Christmas? Well, Believe in the Spirit of Love, Peace, joy, kindness, gentleness all year long.

If distraction comes and a person is bitten by the mosquito, apply therapy. Let the healing begin. Do not turn into a mosquito. Do not allow life to turn you into a viper, predator, or mosquito man. Do not allow circumstances to define you. Let healing begin. Do not perpetuate and turn to the dark side. As you have healed, now is the time to begin again.

Just believe out loud without causing pain. Be careful how you handle others.

"Scholar, Have a Child-like spirit but do not be immature!"

Chapter 12
S - System of Instructions R.O.C

"Everybody is important. Everyone has something to offer."

As a pre-college and college scholar, you can create your own system of instructions to **Rest for Order & Connect.**

Rest and Sleep to Restore:

Sleep deprived story: When I first began taking full-time courses, I was so excited until I stayed up studying or working on assignments for long hours. I made the mistake and mentioned it in a conversation with Dr. Bagayoko. He made it clear that I was to get at least 9 to 10 hours of rest and sleep. Initially, I felt my accomplishments were more important than sleep and my work would be delayed. However, as time progressed, I realized how critical sleep means to a developing brain and to a growing body. Sound wisdom cannot be repudiated or negated. My rest helps me in many ways.

Brain Rest: Absolutely Yes for the body, but THE BRAIN NEEDS REST as well. When knowledge is received, it is received in the short-term memory or the frontal lobe. During the rest or sleep time, the information is transferred to the long-term memory, in the cortex. Because of the vital period of sleep, the brain and the body are given valuable time to transfer knowledge and calibrate. You can gain and retain more knowledge when you rest and sleep following a period of intense learning. Now, I am absolutely a huge advocate of naps during the day and complete sleep throughout the night.

Rest, Relax and Reflect Without Any Devices

Companies Rest: To date there are many corporations which believe and advocate for employee recharging or naps. Some even provide nap rooms for their employees. One company calls the nap area, "Sleeping with the Fishes." This is amazing. The naps have yielded results from better attitudes to overall productivity [9].

God gives Rest - Receive It!: The scripture tells us, "It is vain for you to rise up early, to sit up late to eat the bread of sorrows: for so he giveth his beloved sleep" Psalm 127:2. It is empty to get little sleep. It may seem to work out initially, but it is not good to sacrifice your rest. It affects attitude, accuracy of information and energy levels. And actually, we retain more information over a longer period when we get our sleep. Procrastination is the reason why many people do not get enough rest, so ordering your day is essential.

Order your day, EVERY DAY:

Balancing your day is also the best approach to be a life-long learner, a scholar. Just imagine a place where your day is mapped out and you get to take a nap. When I have a vision for my day, it enhances my specific purpose and direction. Little by little, I experience accomplishments towards my goals rather than cramming everything into one or two long nights.

In my introduction to Engineering course with Dr. Karen Crosby, I acquired some great knowledge about the 60-hour rule for college scholars. For the given credit hours during the semester, there is an allotted amount of time needed for reading, studying, and reviewing information. In short, it is a strategic map to keep a healthy schedule to avoid exhaustion.

When my mom was a scholar at Southern University, she would schedule her courses around noonday prayer with the Students for Christ organization. She even made time for nap time. Then, when she started her career, she would have an hour lunch. For 30 minutes, she would nap and 30 minutes, she would eat her prepared lunch. My mom said, this was her way of turning 1 day into 2 days. In some countries, there are 2 hours allocated for lunch or a mid-day hiatus.

Here is my suggested daily regiment:

Within the 6 am hour

> **6** is the number of man:
> You should rise within this hour.

Within the 7 am hour
> **7** is for completion:
> ALL Sleep is complete,
This is the time for prayer, declarations, scripture, stretching and exercise, getting dressed, and mealtime to be complete.

> **Start everyday declaring you are a Scholar!**

Within the hours from 8 am to 11:30 am

8 is for New beginnings:
Focus your schedule on New Course Concepts, Work, Activities, Meetings and Appointments.

Within the hours from 11:30 am to 1:00 noon
Mid-Day Break:
Rest, Relax and Reflect Without Any Devices
and of course, mealtime.

Within the hours from 1:00 pm to 7:00 pm
Time for Course assignments, Review Courses using the Power Law of Human Performance/Study, Continue Work, Activities, Meetings, and mealtime.

Within the hours from 7:00 pm to 9:00 pm
Time for Final reviews, assess accomplishments,
Preparation and Planning
for the next day
(**9** is for Promotion and advancement, Get your rest).

Within the hours from 9:00 pm to 6:00 am
<u>Rest</u> through Sleep to Restore.

Your schedule may change or be altered but try to maintain a schedule to work towards your holistic goals. I have been told, there are 12 whole hours in the day to get a great deal accomplished. Map it out and create optional schedules that are flexible. Setup short term tasks you can complete and always mark your accomplishments.

A PRODIGY
MY SECRETS AT SOUTHERN UNIVERSITY AND AGRICULTURAL & MECHANICAL COLLEGE, YEAR ONE

"If someone is bored, their imagination is broken."

Connect *for Consistent Networking:*

Professors

You can learn from all those who are put in your path. What to do and what not to do. Everybody's life has a story and an important lesson to learn. Everybody is important. Everyone has something to offer.

Everybody is part of your system of network. If you want to network, you must look the part as well as be the part. Doors of opportunity are given through people. Remember your teachers will have to write letters of recommendation for you. So, if you do not look like you are serious about learning and interacting with your professor, your chances of getting a good letter of recommendation are Ultra-slim. This leaves you skating on thin ice. Connect with your professors in a respectful manner, always.

Professionals

As aforementioned, with opportunities: remember to be a part of research, internships, leadership conferences, professional presentation conferences, university graduate school summits and study abroad opportunities. When given an internship whether paid or volunteer, work experience is work experience. Stay in direct communication with those you meet by providing thank you letters, updates of your status letters, company shadowing visits and corporate office tours.

Peers

Do not let people fool you into acting inappropriately. Your peers may be a door of opportunity as well. They may have interned with a company or maybe in a position looking for new hires. If they bring the wrong person to the company, it may discredit their reputation. Make sure you are always making right choices whether you are around professors, professionals, peers or not. Show yourself to be trustworthy and engaging with people who maybe from a different background. Be sure your appearance, and the way you behave provides chances of succeeding along with that person who was your classmate. You must be the part before you become apart. Be the person who dresses for success. Dress for where you want to go by eliminating certain items of clothing when you attend class. Try to eliminate such items as durags, nightcaps, pajama pants, pajama T-shirts, sagging pants, socks with slippers. Try your best to dress for success each day.

Do not be that person who invests in a lot of fashions, clothing, and shoes, but does not invest in the present and future with professional attire. Buy what you need for your professional career while you are in college. In the words of Pastor Bill "Smith" LeVias of St. Paul Church in Oakland, California, "I have not seen so many people who buy what they want and beg for what they need."

It is said that fashion goes full circle. We can expect to see historically black colleges and universities with elite dress and higher standards in appearance. Making right choices must be demonstrated in all areas of our lives. The ability to make right decisions is what corporations see most appealing. In homeschool, I had to dress for success so I knew my standards would be higher in college.

Create your own System of Instructions:

REST for Sweet Sleep,

ORDER Your day AND

CONNECT WITH Professors, Professionals and Peers.

> *"Nothing a person does in themselves is great unless the people around them get involved."*

"Scholar, Properly <u>Connect</u>, <u>Order</u> Your Day, <u>Rest</u> appropriately and <u>Expect</u> only the Best!"

Gold Bricks from Proverbs
to remember for INSTRUCTIONS:

Listen to advice and accept instruction, that you may gain wisdom in the future. Proverbs 19:20

Keep hold of **instruction**: do not let go; guard her, for she is your life. Proverbs 4:13

Whoever heeds **instruction** is on the path to life, but he who rejects reproof leads others astray. Proverbs 10:17

Whoever loves discipline loves knowledge, but he who hates reproof is stupid. Proverbs 12:1

Hear **instruction** and be wise, and do not neglect it. Proverbs 8:33

The fear (Honor) of God is the beginning of knowledge; fools despise wisdom and **instruction**. Proverbs 1:7

Whoever ignores **instruction** despises himself, but he who listens to reproof gains intelligence. Proverbs 15:32

To receive **instruction** in wise dealing, in righteousness, justice, and equity. Proverbs 1:3

Good sense is a foundation of life to him who has it, but **instruction** of fools is folly. Proverbs 16:22

Cease to hear **instruction**, my son, and you will stray from the words of knowledge. Proverbs 19:27

Give **instruction** to a wise man, and he will be still wiser; teach a righteous man, and he will increase in learning. Proverbs 9:9

ELIJAH J. D. PRECCIELY

My prayer for you

I pray God will grace you with the patience and endurance to allow you to learn and that you will embrace knowledge at an accelerated pace.

I pray you will follow instructions with accuracy and precision.

I pray every obstacle that would stop or block learning for you has been removed.

I pray you will commit to studying and you will be encouraged to know you have the capability to learn.

I pray you will ask the right questions and understand what is available for you.

I pray that all the tools and resources you will need for learning is being allocated to you now.

I pray you will not only understand, but you will provide an understanding heart towards others as they embark on their journey to learn.

I pray you will have a Godly understanding of integrity and ethics that make a difference in the right way to impact lives.

I pray you will grasp on-going technology to advance your education and incorporate technology in every area of your learning.

I pray you will be the catalyst for change and that your change will improve your life and the lives of others.

I pray you will seize every opportunity and benefit from each opportunity.

I pray you will see a vision of yourself learning and advancing your knowledge.

I pray you will take initiative to plan for your rest, schedule and connect with others.

Repeat this prayer, Lord, increase my mental capacity for knowledge and my understanding so I may learn the mysteries of your world.

The Prayer of Salvation

Dear Lord Jesus, I know that I am a sinner, and I ask for Your forgiveness. I believe You died for my sins and rose from the dead. I turn from my sins and invite You to come into my heart, life and fill me with Your precious Holy Spirit. I want to trust and follow You as my Lord and Savior. Amen.

ELIJAH J. D. PRECCIELY

<u>Final Instruction *Scholar*</u>: *Remember the best way to learn is with* **Faith and Love**!

References

[1] Diamond Butler/Southern Digest "Southern University's Founders," Student Media Southern University, November 5, 2019

[2] Rocelyn Hamilton/Digest "History of Southern University," Student Media Southern University, Be Honest, Be Heard, Be History http://www.southerndigest.com/news/article_a5d7e36e-a844-11e7-8094-83625035ff04.html October 3, 2017

[3] Karla Rixon "Southern University [New Orleans] (1956 -)" BlackPast https://www.blackpast.org/african-american-history/southern-university-1880/

[4] George W. Carver, Department of Research and Experiment Station: The Tuskegee Normal and Industrial Institute, Tuskegee, Alabama, "Discovering George Washington Carver — A Man of Character," https://www.nps.gov/gwca/learn/education/upload/Character%20Education%20Book%20Grade%202-4.pdf p24 January 9, 1922

[5] Kennison "Four Categories of knowledge," https://kennison.name/files/tiddly/notes/Four_Types_of_Knowledge.html 2001

[6] Jeff Bennett, "Focus on education: Hints on how to succeed in College Classes" The Astronomical Society of the Pacific

https://purcell.ssl.berkeley.edu/~korpela/astro10/courseinf/success.html 2000

[7] Diola Bagayoko "THE LAW OF HUMAN PERFORMANCE OR OF PRACTICE," http://www.subr.edu/assets/subr/HonorsCollege/pdf/LHP-LawOfHumanPerformance-Font11.5-WithHandbookReference-2018.pdf 2010.

[8] Dr. Maurice Dongier "The Brain from top to Bottom," Canadian Institutes of Health Research: Institute of Neurosciences, Mental Health and Addiction; Douglas Hospital Research Centre https://thebrain.mcgill.ca/flash/d/d_07/d_07_cr/d_07_cr_tra/d_07_cr_tra.html January 2002

[9] Dan Ketchum "You Can Nap on the Job at These 10 Companies," https://finance.yahoo.com/news/nap-job-10-companies-100300632.html February 5, 2019

Biblical references are all scripture quotations from the Holy Bible, King James Version unless otherwise identified.

About the Author

As a result of the grace of God, visionary leadership, the love and support of his family, friends, and university,

Elijah Precciely became a full-time college scholar by 11 years of age. He is the YOUNGEST recipient of the Southern University and Agricultural & Mechanical College's Joseph S. Clark Scholars Award in history. Elijah concentrates his studies in the areas of Physics and Mechanical Engineering.

Community and Leaders:
Elijah's accomplishments have allowed him the recognition and honor by The Governor of Louisiana - Governor John Bel Edwards; The Mayor of Baton Rouge - Mayor-President

Sharon Weston-Broome; The Baton Rouge Metro City Council; Louisiana Senators - Led by Senator Regina Barrow; Louisiana House of Representatives - Led by Representative Edward C. "Ted" James and Paula Davis; and Business Entrepreneurs, Mr. Percy "Master P." Miller and Mr. Romeo Miller at the Essence Festival.

Featured or Highlighted:

Elijah expressly appreciates being a part of reports and articles to inspire and impact the lives of others:
He gives special thanks to WBRZ and ABC News; Afro World Louisiana, Atlanta Black Star, BET Noted Network, Cartoon Network, Christian Life Today Magazine, D. L. Hughley Show, Diversity Inc., Ebony Magazine, Essence Magazine, Good Morning America, HBCU Digest, Idaho Jankins Comedian, JAM Session Weekdays, Prez Blackmon-Song Writer, Ricky Smiley Morning Show, The Advocate, The Root: 2019 Young Futurist, WAFB and CBS News, WGMB and FOX, and many others.

Academic Accomplishments:

At the age of 12, Elijah Precciely was extremely elated to be the youngest inducted into the Southern University Delores Margaret Richard Spikes' Honors College, The Louisiana Collegiate Honors Council (LCHC). The National Association of African American Honors Programs (NAAAHP). The Southern Regional Honors Council (SRHC); and The National Collegiate Honors Council (NCHC) and the SU Dean's list.

Community Outreach:

With great excitement, Elijah participated in the "Drawn to Series" with Cartoon Network to encourage and inspire others to do what they are drawn to that will have a great impact on others. Elijah is the Founder of the G.L.O.W. for Knowledge Challenge (Giving Life-Long Learners Opportunities of Wealth)

Outreach Program. Empowering youth from the cradle to college to increase in knowledge. He also continues to work on more projects; embraces opportunities to inspire; and uplift his community and especially young people to learn with excitement through courses, workshops, meetings, and conferences regardless of the circumstances.

Research and Development:

Elijah Precciely is excited and engaging with university research opportunities with Accredited Doctorate Professors in five main areas: Physics, Agriculture, Biology, Chemistry, and Engineering (Physics and Chemistry with Next Generation Composites Centers for Research in Science and Technology (CREST) with SU and LSU).

Additional works by Elijah J. D. Precciely:
Author of **Mission Christian: God's Got Firsts!**
Talk Show Host of *"Word of Faith"* RadioVision Broadcast

Much more and more to come...including, but not limited to Deuteronomy 28:8 and Ephesians 3:20

Elijah is often asked, why do you continue to do so much at such a young age. His reply is, "I realized very early, I have been trusted with so much. For this purpose, I am grateful."

> Luke 12:28 "To whom much is given much is required" or in the words from the spider man movie, "With great power comes great responsibility."
> I love to give, share, impact and to be a blessing to others everywhere I go.

Thank you all for your kindness, prayers, assistance, and support during this journey!
Visit the author's website at www.AProdigyTheBook.com

www.ingramcontent.com/pod-product-compliance
Lightning Source LLC
Chambersburg PA
CBHW071439160426
43195CB00013B/1960